Contents

CHAPTER FOUR

Recipes

Every recipe you need from starting on solids to feeding a pre-school child

CHAPTER FIVE

Food Scares

Parent Action on everything from patulin in apple juice to BSE, salmonella, pesticides, sex hormones in soya formula and so on . . .

The right diet matters for you and your baby's health.
But in order to develop, your baby also needs
love and emotional nourishment, kindness and tenderness,
play and spiritual guidance. Learning about food is part of
learning about the world in which babies find themselves.
It is an exploration of taste, texture, colour, sight, sound
and smell. Enjoy experiencing these discoveries afresh
with your baby.

ABC

Introduction
Why the right diet matters

The effect of diet on human health has been recognised for centuries, but the science of food and nutrition is relatively new. It was, for example, only in the twentieth century that vitamins were discovered and vitamin deficiencies were recognised as the cause of rickets and scurvy which blighted so many children's lives. We are now witnessing another scientific leap forward as more evidence comes to light that the nutritional status of parents before conception, the mother's diet during pregnancy and breastfeeding, and the food on to which a baby is weaned can 'programme' a child's development and health for the next fifty years.

This book is about getting the balance right from pre-conception to weaning. It offers advice on the best diet for pregnant and nursing mothers and is also a practical guide to weaning and feeding babies and toddlers. By making the right food choices you can help your children develop their full potential in terms of learning, behaviour and general health. And as the chance of your baby developing high blood pressure, heart disease, some cancers, obesity and diabetes in adulthood is linked to poor diet or lifestyle from conception to weaning, you can also help reduce these risks.

At this point sceptical readers will make the observation that children have never been bigger, taller, healthier and better nourished, so why bother about what they eat as babies and toddlers?

The answer is that, while they may be eating enough (or even too many) calories, a comprehensive national survey of the diet and nutrition of British children aged one and a half to four and a half shows that the vast majority do not have a 'healthy diet'. They are eating far too much fat and sugar, and virtually all have soft drinks instead of water, milk or (diluted) fruit juice. They are consuming more chocolate, more confectionery, more sugar, more chips, more biscuits, more savoury snacks, and more sausages and other fatty foods than are good for them. Only 10 per cent eat fish other than in battered deep-fried form or as fish fingers. Few have enough vegetables and fruit: only 25 per cent eat citrus fruit such as oranges, while less than half eat apples, pears or bananas. Not surprisingly, vitamin and mineral intakes are below the ideal – one in eight children in Britain aged one and a half to two and a half years today is anaemic, a condition caused by iron or vitamin B deficiency.

All this goes to show that appearances can be deceptive; British children may be larger than ever, but size is no guarantee of future health and fitness. It is time to teach our pre-school children much better eating habits so that they do not keep Britain near the top of the international league tables for heart disease, cancer and all the other health problems caused by our modern diet and lifestyle.

Diet in pregnancy and your baby

The newly discovered importance of a good diet in pregnancy is that it will reduce the likelihood of low birth weight (2.2 kg/5lb and less), which is linked to health problems later in life. In fact, diet during pregnancy and breastfeeding may have more effect on your baby's adult body size and health than your baby's own genetic constitution does.

Many medical papers have been published to show that people who had a birth weight at the lower end of the normal range have raised blood pressure later in life. Raised blood pressure increases the risk of stroke and heart attack. Differences in the blood pressure of lower birth weight babies show up from as early as five years. These babies are also more likely to develop insulin-dependent diabetes.

Low birth weight is associated with slightly lower IQ and poorer mental performance in early childhood, but this does disappear later in life. In determining mental performance in adults, fetal growth seems to be less important than genetic factors and environmental influences in post-natal life. The brain in the developing fetus (and baby) is usually spared if there is a shortage nutrients for any period in the womb, and growth of other organs is affected first – hence the compromises that occur in other areas of health described above.

Can diet influence IQ?

Intelligence quotient (IQ for short) is mainly determined by the genes you inherit from your parents, particularly your mother. Genes which determine intelligence are mostly located on the X chromosome.

Women have two X chromosomes; men only have one. Women suffer less retardation because they inherit two X chromosomes, one from each parent. If a mutant gene on an X chromosome is inherited there is a good chance that a normal gene on the other X chromosome will compensate, diluting the impact of the mutation.

The Y chromosome is much smaller than the X chromosome, and therefore cannot match every gene on the X chromosome. Any mutant genes on a man's X chromosome can go unopposed and have a full effect. This is why both mental retardation and extraordinary intelligence are more common in men. (See also page 107.)

Growth of the embryo during the eight weeks after conception depends on adequate nutrients and oxygen. Without these the fetus slows its rate of cell division, especially in tissues and organs in their 'critical' periods of growth. Even a brief interruption of nutrition may permanently change the developing tissues and organs, thus 'programming' ill health in adult life. It is thought that many human fetuses (the embryo becomes a fetus at nine weeks) have to adapt to limited supply of nutrients, and in doing so they permanently alter their organs and metabolism. It is these changes and low rates of growth before birth, resulting in low birth weight and in small or disproportionate size, which may increase the rate of death from coronary heart disease (CHD) in adult life and the incidence of related diseases such as stroke, diabetes and high blood pressure. However premature birth, which invariably means low birth weight, does not necessarily result in an increase of CHD.

The risk of diabetes is also increased in people who were small at birth and obese as adults, e.g. some people from the Indian sub-continent who emigrated to Britain. It seems that poor fetal growth reduces the number of pancreatic cells which make insulin, and leads to the body becoming resistant to its own insulin. Thinness at birth is particularly related to insulin resistance later in life, which in turn is associated with diabetes, raised blood pressure and disturbed cholesterol metabolism which leads to CHD. Short babies seem to suffer long-term effects of impaired liver development.

Studies of the relationship between diet during pregnancy and birth weight also suggest that women whose diets in early pregnancy are high in carbohydrates (sugar more so than starches), produce smaller placentas and lighter babies. In late pregnancy low intakes of animal protein (meat and milk) in relation to carbohydrate were also associated with smaller babies. However, these findings need to be confirmed in other studies before any changes are made in dietary advice in pregnancy.

The great importance of diet before conception and during pregnancy does not mean that healthy eating and lifestyle are unimportant during childhood and adult life – they remain essential for enhancing vitality, health and prevention of disease. It is more that the importance of the mother and baby's diet has not previously been fully recognised.

The weaning diet and your baby

Teaching your baby or toddler good eating (and lifestyle) habits is a generous gift that lasts a lifetime. Starting early is important, as there seem to be critical or sensitive phases in early development that have life-long effects on health. For example, the longer the introduction of solid foods is delayed after four months, the more difficult it may become. Introduction after six months might lead to a baby accepting only a restricted range of foods.

New studies show that the taste for a wide variety of food is established early on, during a baby's first six months. Studies show that if you give a baby younger than six months sweetened water or other sweet drinks, he or she will prefer sweet drinks to water at six months through to two years. Studies also demonstrate that in older children, from three to six years old, a taste for crisps and other savoury snacks and over-salted food can develop: these children like over-salted soup, but do not like equally salted water. So children learn to accept tastes in the appropriate context. If you start sprinkling sugar over your baby's breakfast cereal and smothering vegetables in butter (neither is recommended), then he or she will not learn to accept those foods without these extras. The child may be programmed to go on to eat a high sugar, high fat diet, with all the implications for diet-related diseases later in life. It has also been known for a long time that the human race has an innate preference for sweet-tasting food – this can be demonstrated in newborns. It probably developed during evolution because sweet tastes are associated with high calorie (and non-toxic) foods, which were important to Stone Age people for whom food was scarce.

If you wean babies on to a restricted number of foods and tastes, they may end up liking only a limited number of foods later on. Conversely if you introduce very young children between four and six months to a much wider range of food they learn to like a much wider range of food. And the cornerstone of healthy eating through-out life is to enjoy a wide range of foods, because this provides a wide range of nutrients (vitamin and minerals). The younger they start, the easier it is for children to develop a taste for a balanced

diet. Delaying weaning may miss this window of opportunity and result in a faddy eater who likes only a limited number of bland foods. Similarly, delaying the introduction of different-textured foods at appropriate times during weaning (up to one year) may result in your baby persisting with a bottle for too long and consequently delaying development of chewing and speaking mechanisms.

Despite accepted wisdom that babies like bland food, they have been shown to enjoy stronger flavours too. But children differ in their sensitivity to flavour. Some studies suggest that pre-school children with low taste sensitivity tend to accept more foods and have more enthusiasm for them than children with the highest taste sensitivity. This suggests that it is a good idea to offer tasty food early on in weaning, because food preferences too are established within the first year; and you want your baby to like a wide range of tasty foods because a healthy diet is a varied diet.

Accustoming babies during weaning to 'eating up greens' should also pre-empt later battles of wills. If babies are introduced to lots of vegetables early on they are more likely to accept them as a normal part of their diet, and parents will not have to wear themselves out cajoling older babies and toddlers to eat their vegetables.

Familiarity is a strong influence which parents can put to positive or negative use. From weaning to adolescence, children prefer foods in the form and texture with which they are familiar. New foods are more likely to be rejected on sight alone after two years of age. Children have by then learned to like specific foods in particular forms over and above the flavour of the food. Whether they try new foods after this age will be determined by social factors such as imitation of other children and family and social reinforcement – mainly in the home. So over to you!

Like mother like daughter

Eating problems may be passed on from mothers to children. The babies of mothers who are highly restrained in what they eat, or who have eating disorders, are more likely to fail to thrive than those born to mothers with a 'normal' attitude to their body shape and weight. Some babies' poor weight gain can be caused by diet and not disease, when mothers restrict the food they give to their children. In many cases, such mothers restrict what they would wrongly consider to be 'unhealthy' or 'fattening' foods. Most of these mothers describe mealtimes as tense, with battles over food intake. Relationship problems between parents, maternal depression and anxiety, parenting difficulties, clinical conditions such as maternal anorexia nervosa or bulimia nervosa (estimated as affecting one in every hundred women), and (though rarely) putting a child on a restricted vegan diet are to blame.

CHAPTER 1

Pregnancy

Your guide to eating well for you and your baby

There are many good reasons for eating a 'healthy' diet before and during pregnancy – not least of which is the pure enjoyment of good food. Research suggests that babies whose mothers eat a well-balanced diet are less likely to be low birth weight, which, as we have seen, reduces the risk of common health problems in adulthood.

A well-balanced diet also provides the mother with lots of energy and helps keep her weight gain in check. Average weight gain during pregnancy is between 10 and 15kg (20–30lb). This is made up, approximately, of 3–4kg (6–8lb) weight of baby, and 7–17kg (14–24lb) for placenta, amniotic fluid, increased blood, fluid, fat and breast tissue. Pregnancy is not the time to be worrying about weight gain and you should never diet (that is, slim) during pregnancy except on medical advice.

From conception to birth

Your diet before and during pregnancy will affect the health of your baby. The most critical stage is just before and after conception. Different terms are used to describe the stages of development of your baby during pregnancy.

Your baby is *pre-embryonic (days 0–14 post-conception)* when the fertilised egg is transported down the fallopian tube to the uterus, where it implants. During this time cell division, which relies on good nutrition to be successful, occurs, and by the second week the cells have differentiated to form the beginnings of the embryo.

Your baby is an *embryo (weeks 3–8 post-conception)* when three basic layers are formed from which the organs and tissues develop. The central nervous system is one of the first to develop – hence the need for folic acid supplements before and early in pregnancy. The heart, blood vessels and brain are also developing, the limbs are budding and you can recognise the eyes and nose. It is at this early stage that too much vitamin A can produce severe physical and mental defects.

Your baby is then a *fetus (week 9 to birth)*. At this stage the placenta takes over supplying nutrients and oxygen to your baby. Before that time the embryo relies for its nutrients on whatever is circulating in your blood – there is no placenta to screen out substances or protect your baby from deficiencies. Some organs such as those of the urogenital system continue to be formed, but the main development consists of growth of already formed structures and development of normal functions.

Healthy diet before pregnancy

The ideal way to give your baby the best start in life is for both partners to enjoy a healthy diet and lifestyle before conceiving a baby: give up smoking and greatly reduce or cut out alcohol and check with your doctor whether medicines or drugs you are using can affect an unborn baby. Obviously the longer you have been well nourished the better, but for those anxious to start a family a four-month overhaul of diet and lifestyle would benefit your baby-to-be. And that really does mean dads

too, because damaged sperm can lead to birth defects. Check the safety of medicines and drugs with your GP for pregnancy and pre-pregnancy.

What is a healthy diet in pregnancy?

A good diet in pregnancy is much the same as at any other time; in other words it means enjoying a wide variety of foods in the right proportion (see below). In addition during pregnancy you need to eat safely (see the information on foods to avoid on page 25) and before conception, or once you conceive, take folic acid supplements (see page 21). Contrary to popular belief, you need not eat any more than the 1940 calories a day recommended for a non-pregnant adult woman (teenagers need 2110 as they are still growing). An extra 200 calories a day during the last trimester (weeks 27 to 40) is the only additional food you need. Of course, if you are very active you may need more food. However, because your baby needs a good supply of vitamins and minerals you need to ensure that the food you eat is 'nutrient-dense'. This means avoiding so-called junk foods which are high in fat and sugar – supplying lots of calories – but low in vitamins and minerals.

Pregnancy and breastfeeding eating plan

Food	Daily servings
Bread, pasta, potatoes, rice, other cereals	Four, or more if hungry
Vegetables and fruit	Five, or more if hungry
Milk and milk products	Three (four if needed when breast-feeding)
Lean meat, poultry, fish, vegetarian alternatives	Two to three
Fats for cooking and spreading	Small amounts
Sugary and fatty foods e.g. confectionery, pies and biscuits	Limited treats, not to replace foods

Getting the balance right

The eating plan shows the proportions of each food group needed for a balanced diet. New studies also show that, if your diet is out of proportion at different stages of pregnancy, that too can affect your baby's weight. For example, a low birth weight (under 2.2kg/5lb) was associated with high carbohydrate intake in early pregnancy and low dairy or meat protein intake in late pregnancy. So eating a varied and well-balanced diet at all times is important.

Nutrient-dense food groups

STARCHY FOODS

Bread, pasta, breakfast cereal (without any/much added sugar/salt/chocolate/honey), potatoes, rice, oats, noodles, grains (millet, maize, cornmeal). Choose high fibre versions whenever possible, and cook and serve them without much added fat. These starchy foods (together with vegetables and fruit) should form the main part of all meals since they provide energy, fibre and nutrients. Eat a minimum of four servings a day, five if you are breastfeeding.

VEGETABLES AND FRUIT

Eat at least five servings daily, whether fresh, frozen or canned (avoid brine/syrup), cooked or raw. Choose green and orange fruit and vegetables for antioxidant vitamins and minerals. Enjoy salads regularly. Cook and prepare these foods carefully to minimise the loss of vitamins and minerals. Unsweetened fresh fruit juice counts as a serving, but it lacks the fibre and other components of whole fruit – and too much can damage your teeth.

LOW FAT DAIRY FOODS

Milk, cheese, yogurt or other dairy produce. Eat at least three servings a day, more if you are breastfeeding. Calcium from dairy foods is needed for healthy bones and teeth by both mother and baby. After the first three months of pregnancy a baby's teeth begin to form, and during the last three months its bones are being strengthened. Eaten regularly, sardines, watercress and bread are also good sources of calcium.

LOW FAT MEAT, POULTRY, FISH OR VEGETARIAN ALTERNATIVES

Eat two servings a day. Choose fish (especially oily kinds such as salmon, herrings and mackerel) a couple of times a week. Protein is important for the growth of new tissue for you and your baby. If you eat a well-balanced diet that provides enough calories you should obtain enough protein, as the average British woman eats more protein than she needs. Her average intake is 62 grams per day, which is more than the Reference Nutrient Intake (RNI, the amount thought to be enough to cover everybody's needs) of 45g a day. In pregnancy only an extra 6g a day is needed. During breastfeeding up to six months an additional 11g a day is needed, falling to 8g for those who continue to breastfeed after their baby is six months old.

FATS

Altogether a more complicated area! While adults should eat only moderate amounts of fat we should never go on a fat-free diet as some fat (of the right sort) is as vital for health as vitamins and minerals. This is especially important during pregnancy. Choose spreads that are low fat and/or high in polyunsaturates, and eat them sparingly. Use polyunsaturated or monounsaturated oils for cooking/salad dressings/spreading, because everyone needs the essential fatty acids found in vegetable oils (such as sunflower and corn oil), green leafy vegetables, nuts and seeds. 'Essential' fatty acids (fatty acids are the components of fats) are needed so that your body can make the long chain fatty acids which are essential for your baby's brain, eye and nerve development and for cell walls. The long chain fatty acids are also found ready-made in oily fish such as mackerel, herring and salmon. The fetus and newborn baby may not be able to make these long chain fatty acids, so they are obtained from the mother via the placenta and in breastmilk. Studies have shown that women producing lower birth weight babies have lower intakes of essential fatty acids than those mothers who deliver normal weight babies.

It is also better for pregnant women to lay down body fat made from polyunsaturated fats (rather than saturated fats) in preparation for breastfeeding, because fatty acids find their way into breastmilk, and ready-formed long chain polyunsaturated fatty acids are needed by your baby for brain development. It is the absence of the right kind of fatty acids in most artificial baby milk that is thought partially to explain why breastfed babies have higher IQs and better visual acuity. If only the wrong sort of saturated fats are available, these will be substituted in your baby's brain.

The World Health Organisation estimates that 600g/1lb 5oz of essential fatty acids (approximately 2g a day) will be laid down in the normal pregnancy of a well-nourished woman. As women may become less efficient at turning essential fatty acids from vegetable sources into long chain fatty acids during pregnancy, there may be some benefit in eating more oily fish which, as explained, contains ready-made long chain fatty acids. Some studies show that high fish intake reduces both premature birth and pregnancy-associated high blood pressure and results in higher birth-weight babies.

SUGARY OR FATTY FOODS

Limit foods such as crisps, chocolate, cakes, biscuits, fried foods and pies to treats.

DRINK

Aim for at least eight glasses of fluid a day so that your body can manufacture the extra blood needed in pregnancy. Fluid (and starchy fibre-rich foods) also prevent constipation. During breast-feeding you will need to drink at least one litre/1¾ pints a day.

Water, unsweetened fruit juice (diluted, if you like) or milk are the best drinks. Replace some or all of your normal intake of tea, coffee, cola and fizzy/soft drinks with these, or try decaffeinated versions. If you do still drink standard tea and coffee make them weak so as to avoid too much caffeine and tannin (present in tea, coffee, cola and other fizzy drinks, and chocolate), because these are stimulants which can pass to the baby in the uterus and later via breastmilk. They may also make you jittery and edgy. During the last three months of pregnancy your body metabolises caffeine more slowly, so it stays in your system for longer. Tea and coffee are also diuretic, causing loss of water-soluble vitamins. Caffeine will not cause birth defects, and links to miscarriage are inconclusive. Tannin can 'bind' iron, making it unavailable to the body – do not drink tea until at least half an hour after meals. Limit tea and coffee to no more than four weak cups a day.

If you substitute herb or fruit teas for regular tea and coffee avoid those made from celery, cinnamon, parsley and sage during the first three months of pregnancy and while breastfeeding. These herbs and spices can, however, still be used in cooking. For further information contact a qualified medical herbalist or the National Institute of Medical Herbalists (see Useful Addresses page 205). See also page 182.

Eating for two needs only 200 extra calories a day

Two hundred calories can easily be mis-spent on confectionery and other poor-quality snacks. Among the better choices are:
● Two slices wholemeal bread/toast or bagel/roll with low fat cheese

- Jacket potato with 25g/1oz cheese
- One slice cheese on toast
- Wholemeal fruit bun/muffin with low fat spread and preserve/Marmite
- Two medium bananas
- Three or four fish fingers
- Prawn/canned salmon and salad sandwich (no spread/mayonnaise)
- One bowl porridge with a few raisins
- Potato scone/farl with one lean grilled rasher of bacon
- Cup of soup and roll/bread
- Generous 25g/1oz unsalted nuts
- One large oatcake and low fat spread
- One large bowl breakfast cereal (such as Shredded Wheat, Weetabix, muesli) with semi-skimmed milk and fruit
- Glass of milk or low sugar milkshake
- 70g/2½oz hummus with carrot/celery sticks/fingers of pitta bread
- ● One wholemeal fruit bun
- ● Two slices of toasted raisin bread, smear low fat spread
- Small piece of fruit cake, no icing
- 75g/3oz dried fruit (pears, apricots, prunes, peaches, apples)
- One samosa
- Two to three felafels (depending on size)
- Nuts, about 25g/1oz (see also warning on nuts in pregnancy on pages 18 and 169).

SNACK TIP

When buying snack foods, ready meals, canned and packaged foods, read the ingredients label to avoid foods that are full of sugar, modified starch, water and other cheap fillers that lack vitamins and minerals.

Daily menu – eat three meals a day

Regular meals throughout the day are important to provide you and your baby with a constant supply of energy, vitamins and minerals.

BREAKFAST

Without breakfast it is hard to eat enough vitamins and minerals and fibre during the day. Good choices:
- Fruit, plus breakfast cereal fortified with vitamins and minerals, or porridge with skimmed or semi-skimmed milk
- Wholemeal toast, buns or muffins

See also Morning Sickness (page 17).

LUNCH

Choose from:
- Sandwiches from high fibre bread. Vary the fillings to include the leanest meat you can afford, fish (e.g. tuna, salmon; sardines are good because the bones are eaten and provide calcium), hummus and vegetarian options. Add as much salad or watercress as you can or have salad on the side
- Large salad with lean meat/fish/vegetarian alternative and wholemeal roll
- Soup (vegetable, pulses, pasta, with or without lean meat/fish), bread and cheese

FOLLOWED BY
- Fruit or yogurt/fromage frais

MAIN MEAL

Concentrate on protein foods at your main meal. Choose from:
- Lean meat, fish, eggs or vegetarian alternative cooked by a low fat method, e.g. grilled, poached, roasted without additional fat or steamed, served with at least two portions of vegetables and

accompanied by potatoes or pasta or rice or bread. Make frequent use of dark green leafy and orange vegetables, such as all types of cabbage and greens, carrots, pumpkin/squash

- Casseroles extended with pulses. Cook the day before, cool, remove fat and reheat thoroughly
- Home-made burgers, fishcakes, kebabs, shepherds' pie, fish pies with meat/fish extended by addition of grated/diced onion, carrots, potato etc., served as above. Use fresh or canned fish pasta/risotto with vegetables and lean meat/fish/vegetarian alternative

PUDDING

Limit yourself to one a day and try to choose a nutrient-dense dessert such as:

- Fresh (or canned) fruit salad (occasionally with ice cream)
- Dried fruit compote with yogurt
- Bread and butter pudding
- Rice pudding with fruit
- Pancakes with fruit purees
- Lowish sugar fruit crumbles with low fat custard
- Apple strudel (made with filo pastry)
- Real fruit jellies
- Panforte
- Fresh fruit fools with reduced fat cream or Greek yogurt
- Fruit brûlée (made with yogurt, not cream)

Morning sickness

This usually stops after fourteen weeks. It describes nausea or vomiting, and, despite the name, can happen at any time of day. Many women worry that being unable to eat may prevent their baby growing properly. Unless you start a pregnancy undernourished or very underweight, or have severe prolonged sickness, your body's store of nutrients should keep your baby supplied. It may not seem much consolation, but morning sickness is generally a sign of a healthy pregnancy that is far less likely to end in miscarriage.

If you are unable to eat much, what you do eat should be as nutritious as possible. Try plain foods such as mashed potatoes with a little cheese, or chopped vegetables or soup or bread or porridge. If the smell of cooking is a problem, eat sandwiches or yogurt, or fruit or breakfast cereal. If you really cannot eat, sip milk or fruit juice as often as possible and nibble snacks (see 200 calorie choices on page 14).

Eating five or six snack meals a day (e.g. every two to three hours) can be helpful because nausea is often worse when you are hungry. Snack meals are also useful later in pregnancy when indigestion and discomfort after normal-size meals are common. If you do switch to a pattern of snack meals or 'grazing', choose the nutrient-dense snacks (described above) and try to avoid snacks and packaged foods that are full of cheap fillers but lacking in vitamins and minerals.

Should you eat nuts during pregnancy?

It may be wise for atopic pregnant and breastfeeding women (those with a history of allergy) to avoid eating peanuts in order to prevent potentially life-threatening allergies to nuts developing in their babies (see also page 169). Studies show that almost 40 per cent of mothers of children with peanut allergy ate peanuts at least weekly when pregnant or breastfeeding.

Proteins from the 'offending' foods reach the fetus via the mother's blood in early pregnancy and through the placenta in later pregnancy, and reach the baby in breastmilk after birth. The proteins act as allergens (substances that provoke an allergic reaction) when ingested by susceptible babies. Evidence that antibodies have been produced by the fetus has been seen as early as eleven weeks. Even though this is thought to be rare, there is growing concern that sensitisation to peanuts might occur during pregnancy, making the exclusion of nuts from the mother's diet during pregnancy a sensible precaution in atopic families.

The babies most at risk may be those whose mothers already have some form of allergy. Peanut allergy is becoming increasingly common, and the age of children affected is getting lower; the allergy may occur even in the first year. This is probably due to the general increase in allergic disease and early (as early as in the uterus) and increased exposure to peanuts. Peanut allergy is most common among children with other allergic illnesses such as asthma, eczema, hay fever and rhinitis, or where allergy runs in the family. Symptoms include swollen lips and face, wheezing and breathlessness. Anaphylactic shock (or death; see page 172) does not happen on first exposure to peanuts.

Pregnancy for the vegetarian mother

Vegetarians may have a far healthier diet than non-vegetarians, so it is not really fair to single them out for special consideration. However, vegetarians whose only dietary change is to give up meat do need to make more effort! Meat and/or fish need to be replaced by vegetarian sources of protein which fall into three groups:
- Pulses (soya and other beans, chickpeas, lentils, split peas etc.)
- Grains (wheat which makes bread, pasta, or rice and other cereals)
- Nuts and seeds (including peanut and other nut butters)

Meat substitutes such as Quorn, tofu and soya-based foods also supply protein. Combining two of the three vegetarian protein food groups during the day ensures that all nine essential amino acids (protein 'building blocks') are present in the right proportions to fulfil the protein needs of both mother and baby. Dairy foods enhance the available protein in vegetable foods, so vegetarians who eat milk, yogurt, cheese and eggs will obtain complete protein easily. However, vegans (who eat no animal food) need to plan their diet very carefully.

For most women there is no need to worry about protein: as long as you are eating enough calories in a varied diet you will obtain enough. See also Essential Nutrients below, especially the information on iron, B vitamins and calcium, and pages 20, 22, 23.

Essential nutrients: the basics

There are only a few nutrients for which there is an increased need during pregnancy: vitamin A, folic acid, vitamin C, vitamin B2 (riboflavin) and vitamin D. While breastfeeding you will need a small increase on recommended pre-pregnancy levels of several minerals: calcium, phosphorus, magnesium, zinc, copper and selenium, and of vitamins B3 (niacin) and B12.

The slight increase in requirement of these nutrients does not mean that you need to eat large amounts of certain foods. Following the eating plan outlined in this chapter – eating a varied daily diet based on the nutrient-dense foods mentioned – will ensure that you meet recommended intakes. Neither do you have to take a vitamin and mineral supplement. The small increases in need should be covered by eating the nutrient-dense foods recommended earlier, and by replacing fatty and sugary foods that supply only 'empty calories' with more nutritious foods if necessary.

WHEN ARE VITAMIN AND MINERAL SUPPLEMENTS CALLED FOR?

Other than folic acid and prescribed iron (which is not automatically needed in pregnancy), vitamin and mineral supplements are not recommended during pregnancy because too much vitamin A can be toxic (see page 25). However, if a well-balanced diet is not possible, and if lifestyle changes cannot be made (such as giving up smoking and drinking, which both increase the need for vitamins and minerals, from the time you start trying to conceive) or if nausea or sickness are severe, a supplement may be advisable. Check with your family doctor, midwife or other health professional.

If you do take a vitamin and mineral supplement, choose one that provides no more than 100 per cent RDA (Recommended Daily Allowance) to avoid any toxic effect. The largest nutrient needs occur at the beginning and end of pregnancy, so limited use during those times would seem to be the safest option.

Essential nutrients in more detail

FOLIC ACID

Pregnant women are advised to take folic acid tablets for three months before becoming pregnant and through the first three months of pregnancy to reduce the risk of spina bifida, other neural tube defects, and related conditions such as anencephaly (absence of brain at birth) that occur when the neural tube is being formed early in pregnancy. However, as half of pregnancies in the UK are not planned, the next best is to start as soon as you suspect you might be pregnant.

Without daily folic acid tablets of 400 micrograms (mcg) or 0.4 milligrams (mg) daily, which cost between 2p and 4p a day (depending on brand), every baby is potentially at risk. Ninety-five per cent of babies with spina bifida and related conditions are born to first-time mothers or those who have previously had a healthy baby. The risk is the same regardless of the mother's age, state of health, smoking habits or social class, whether she already has healthy children and whether or not there is spina bifida in the family. However, over-weight pregnant mothers are more likely than lean mothers to have a child with spina bifida or anencephaly. In one study this happened even though the mothers took folic acid before and during early pregnancy. In addition to supplements, foods rich in folates (the name given to folic acid where it occurs naturally in food) should also be eaten regularly. There is no danger of overdosing.

GOOD SOURCES (ALL FOODS LISTED IN ORDER OF FOLIC ACID CONTENT PER SERVING)

50–100mcg per average serving:
cooked black eye beans, brussels sprouts, beef and yeast extracts, cooked kidney, kale, spinach, spring greens, broccoli and green beans.
15–50mcg per serving:
cooked soya beans, cauliflower, cooked chickpeas, potatoes, iceberg lettuce, oranges, peas, orange juice, parsnips, baked beans, wholemeal bread, cabbage, yogurt, white bread, eggs, brown rice, wholegrain pasta. Many breads and breakfast cereals are fortified with folic acid.

LIVER WARNING

Although liver is a rich source of folates, it should not be eaten if you are planning a baby or pregnant. See warning page 25.

VITAMIN C

This vitamin is well known for its role in immunity and promoting healing. It is an antioxidant (which means that it offers protection against free radical damage that can precipitate cancer, heart disease and other conditions) and it is needed for healthy blood vessels. It is valuable (especially for vegetarians) for promoting iron absorption during pregnancy, and is needed to build strong muscles, blood vessels and cartilage in your baby. Free radicals are produced constantly in the body as part of the normal function of using oxygen. They are highly reactive and need to be 'mopped up' instantly by antioxidants such as vitamin Cs and E and beta-carotene.

VITAMIN B2 (RIBOFLAVIN)

This and other B vitamins are needed by your body to release energy from food, and for healthy skin.

VITAMIN A

Although too much vitamin A can be dangerous to your unborn baby, you do need slightly more during pregnancy. Vitamin A can be eaten either in the retinol form in which it is found in animal foods, or as beta-carotene which occurs in orange and green fruit and vegetables. Beta-carotene is turned into vitamin A in the body if more of this vitamin is needed; otherwise it acts as an antioxidant (see Vitamin C, above).

VITAMIN D

Supplements may be needed if your diet does not include oily fish, eggs and margarine, or if your skin is very dark and not exposed to natural daylight because of clothing or lifestyle.

Other important nutrients

Some other nutrients are also particularly important before and during pregnancy.

IRON

One of the minerals that is commonly in short supply in the British diet, especially among young women. If you do not get enough iron you will feel tired and may become anaemic. However, you do not need any more than before you became pregnant (so long as this was enough), because during pregnancy your body becomes more efficient at absorbing the iron that you and your baby need. Eating foods rich in iron will help prevent the need for iron supplements, which may be prescribed in pregnancy and can cause constipation. Blood tests for iron status should be taken early in pregnancy, usually at the first ante-natal appointment. The baby also relies on reserves laid down during pregnancy, especially during the baby's first six months of life.

Most vegetarians, with the exception of teenage girls, do not have iron deficiency, but they are theoretically at greater risk. This is because iron from meat is absorbed more easily by the body than iron from vegetable sources. To overcome this, consume vitamin C-rich food or drink (such as citrus fruit and juice, vegetables and fruit) with vegetable sources of iron.

GOOD SOURCES
Lean meat, fortified breakfast cereals, wholemeal bread, green leafy vegetables, dried fruit (figs, apricots, peaches, dates, prunes), nuts and seeds.

CALCIUM

A growing baby makes demands on your reserves of calcium, which need topping up to keep your teeth healthy and to prevent osteoporosis later in life. However, absorption of calcium from food increases when you are pregnant, so there is no need to eat more than

the 700mg a day recommended for non-pregnant women (teenagers need 800mg a day and may need more if they have had a poor diet and are still growing). Adequate calcium may also help prevent pregnancy-induced high blood pressure and its more serious form, life-threatening pre-eclampsia. Some US health experts are lobbying for official recommendation for calcium supplements (similar to folic acid recommendations), although there is opposition from the dairy industry which would rather people ate their calcium than took it as tablets.

GOOD SOURCES

Low fat milk, yogurt, fromage frais, cheese, canned fish with edible bones (pilchards, salmon, sardines). Vegetarians should choose calcium-fortified soya products such as tofu and soya milk. Fresh vegetable juice, broccoli, almonds, sesame seeds and tahini are popular choices with vegetarians.

ESSENTIAL FATS

Although fats and fatty foods should be eaten sparingly, small amounts of some polyunsaturated fats are essential for the baby's brain, eye, nerve and other development. Fish, especially oily kinds such as mackerel, herring and salmon, contain these long chain fatty acids. Eat fish a couple of times a week. But do not worry if you are vegetarian or cannot eat fish, because similar fatty acids in green leafy vegetables and vegetable oils (also found in margarine/spread) can be turned into long chain versions by your body so long as other nutrients are available in a balanced diet. Beware of fish oil supplements, which may contain too much vitamin A (see page 25 for a list of foods to avoid when you are pregnant).

VITAMIN E

Low levels of vitamin E have been associated with low birth weight. The main source of vitamin E in the UK diet is vegetable oil and fats, for instance margarine made from it or fortified with it. Vitamin E is needed for fertility; it is also an antioxidant and is necessary for building blood vessels, for muscles and to keep the immune system working. The average UK intake for women is 6.7mg a day. A traditional Mediterranean diet, the vitamin E content of which is thought to help protect against heart disease, provides about 30mg a day. Antioxidant experts think we probably need between 80 and 100mg a day. Protection against angina in a medical study at Cambridge was achieved using 400mg a day. However, the UK government has no Reference Nutrient Intake (the amount of a vitamin or mineral that is enough for almost everyone, even those with high needs) for vitamin E. Under EC labelling law, which applies to British foods, the RDA (Recommended Daily Allowance) is 10mg a day, but obviously from the figures quoted above this amount bears no relation to actual requirements.

VITAMIN B12

This vitamin is not in short supply among meat and fish eaters, and it is unlikely to be a problem for vegetarians who eat dairy foods regularly. Vegans, however, may need a supplement (although a wide range of foods (such as soya milk, yeast extract, breakfast cereal, textured vegetable protein and other specialist vegetarian and vegan foods are already supplemented with B12). B12 (with folic acid) has an important role in the production of genetic material called DNA, which is constantly produced during growth of your baby. It is also needed to help prevent anaemia and for healthy blood.

Safe eating: foods to avoid during pregnancy

LIVER

This meat contains up to twenty times the Recommended Daily Allowance of vitamin A because farmers feed it to livestock as a growth promoter. Too much vitamin A can cause serious birth defects, so avoid eating liver just before and during pregnancy. You

will not go short of vitamin A, because the body can turn beta-carotene found in orange and green fruit and vegetables into vitamin A if it is needed. Also avoid liver pâté and sausage. Liver and liver products are safe for non-pregnant breastfeeding women.

PÂTÉ, RIPENED SOFT CHEESES (E.G. CAMEMBERT AND BRIE) AND BLUE-VEINED CHEESE

These foods should be avoided as high levels of listeria bacteria have been found in them. Listeriosis is a rare illness producing no more than flu-like symptoms in pregnant women but severely affecting a developing baby, resulting in stillbirth or severe illness in newborns. Listeria can also occur in cook-chill meals, but reheating them thoroughly to piping hot will destroy the bacteria. Vegetables and salads (including ready-washed) may contain listeria too, so wash them carefully.

RAW EGGS OR FOODS MADE WITH UNCOOKED OR UNDERCOOKED EGG (E.G. SCRAMBLED EGG, OMELETTES, ICE CREAM, FRESHLY MADE MAYONNAISE, SOME DIPS, COLD SOUFFLÉS AND MOUSSES)

All these should be avoided as they may contain salmonella, which may result in food poisoning (sickness and diarrhoea) in the mother; however, it rarely causes damage to unborn babies. Like eggs, poultry and meat should be cooked thoroughly to destroy salmonella bacteria. Frozen poultry needs to be defrosted completely before cooking or reheating to ensure it reaches high enough temperatures during cooking to destroy bacteria. Take care to wash your hands after handling raw poultry and meat. Store raw meat separately from cooked, preferably on a lower shelf in the fridge so that any dripping juices will not cause contamination, and use different utensils for preparation. Commercially produced mayonnaise in jars is made with pasteurised egg and can be eaten safely. Some shops sell pasteurised liquid and dried egg.

RAW OR UNDERCOOKED (RARE) MEAT

These should not be eaten in case they contain food poisoning bacteria and the parasite that causes toxoplasmosis, an illness that can be passed to unborn babies and cause miscarriage or serious brain and eye damage. Always wash your hands after touching raw meat and poultry.

UNPASTEURISED GOAT'S AND SHEEP'S MILK AND CHEESE

The toxoplasmosis parasite has also been found in these foods, as well as in soil and cat faeces: this is another reason to wash vegetables and salads thoroughly. Wash your hands after touching kittens and cats, especially when cleaning out litter trays (use rubber gloves, or get someone else to do it for you). Also, wear gloves for gardening.

RAW (UNTREATED) GREEN TOP MILK

Whether cow's, goat's or sheep's, this may contain bacteria and other organisms that can cause illness, so avoid drinking it during pregnancy.

SHELLFISH

Oysters, prawns, mussels, crabs and so on should only be eaten if cooked thoroughly. In their raw state they may contain harmful bacteria and viruses.

ALCOHOL

Best avoided when you are trying to conceive and during early pregnancy because it creates risks to fetal and early infant development. If you do drink, limit yourself to one or two units once or twice a week and avoid getting drunk. The normal low risk level for women (e.g. the upper weekly limit of 14 units, recently revised by the government to 21 but not accepted by doctors) does not apply during pregnancy. Neither does the 'protective' effect of a low intake of alcohol against heart disease apply during pregnancy; it is really only valuable for post-menopausal women.

As a general rule, one unit of alcohol equals:
- 1 pub measure of spirits i.e. ⅙th gill, 25 ml, 1 fl oz
- 1 small glass wine i.e. 125 ml, 4 fl oz
- ½ pint or 300 ml ordinary strength beer, cider or lager
- 125 ml, ¼ pint strong beer, cider or lager
- 1 small glass sherry i.e. 80 ml, 2¾ fl oz

In some States in America pregnant women can be prosecuted for endangering the life of their babies if they drink alcohol.

Diabetes and diet in pregnancy

Women with well-controlled insulin dependent diabetes are just as fertile as other women, and just as capable of having a healthy, happy pregnancy. However, pregnancy will be slightly harder work than for women without diabetes because of the planning and preparation required to keep blood sugar levels constant.

The ideal way to start is to visit a pre-pregnancy clinic at your local hospital. Good control in very early pregnancy is important because, as already explained, the new baby is completely formed in the first three months. At the clinic you will be advised to carry out more frequent blood glucose monitoring than normal. When you and your doctor agree that your HbA1 (the test that averages out the peaks and troughs of your blood glucose level over the last two to three months and gives an accurate indication of your diabetes control) is satisfactory, then you should stop contraception. If there is no local pre-pregnancy clinic ask your doctor to refer you to the obstetrician who will be looking after you, or ask for your HbA1 to be checked.

If possible, combine a visit to your diabetes doctor with hospital ante-natal visits. Many diabetic women are naturally concerned

about hypos during their pregnancy. Make sure you have a good supply of sugary foods to hand in case of emergencies, and ensure that your partner or whoever is looking after you has glucagon (a hormone that regulates blood-glucose) to hand and knows how to use it. That said, hypos cannot damage a baby. But ketones can if they build up over several hours. If your blood glucose is high, if you are vomiting or are ill, test for ketones and tell your doctor immediately if more than a small amount is present. If morning sickness is a problem take more carbohydrate (even fluid) and test for ketones.

The amount of insulin needed may increase from about week 24. After thirty weeks your pregnancy will be monitored more closely, and you may need to decide on an earlier delivery.

See also Useful Addresses.

Gestational diabetes

This term describes diabetes that is first diagnosed during pregnancy. It occurs because pregnancy increases the need for insulin, and in some pregnant women the pancreas does not produce extra insulin. Being overweight increases the need for insulin, which makes overweight women more at risk of gestational diabetes.

Most women with this condition need do no more than stop eating sweet foods and choose a healthy diet. However, if home tests show that even on a healthy diet blood glucose levels are just as high, insulin will be needed for the rest of the pregnancy. Many women find they can stop insulin (under medical supervision) after the birth of their babies, when their bodies are making enough insulin for non-pregnancy needs.

Cravings

A desire for particular foods or unusual combinations is not thought to be related to nutritional deficiencies. Surveys of foods commonly

craved during pregnancy do not seem to differ greatly from foods that women crave when they are not pregnant – such as chocolate and crisps! Other common cravings are for spicy food, ice cream, onions and pickles.

Exercise

In conjunction with eating well, it is important to stay active during pregnancy. But this does not mean taking up strenuous exercise if you were inactive before. Start gently, and try to exercise regularly either with daily walks of around 30 minutes or three exercise sessions a week. Any amount is better than nothing. Remember to drink plenty in hot weather and during or after exercise. If you go to exercise classes, ensure that the teacher is properly qualified and let him or her know that you are pregnant so that any necessary modifications can be pointed out to you during the class. Keeping up regular exercise during pregnancy will help you get back into shape more quickly after the birth of your baby.

Teenage pregnancy

Young girls who find themselves pregnant and living on benefit support will have very limited budgets for food, and probably not very good cooking facilities. But they still need 2110 calories a day to meet both their own growth and that of their baby. Ask your doctor to refer you to a dietitian who will help you plan a nutritious but affordable diet.

THE ABC OF HEALTHY EATING FOR BABIES AND TODDLERS

CHAPTER TWO

Breastfeeding

Your baby's diet from birth to four months

For the first few months of life, babies require only breastmilk. Although this is the best food in the world for babies until they are weaned, one of the first 'decisions' that parents, especially mothers, have to face is whether to breast- or bottle-feed their new baby. Many considerations influence this choice: partners, immediate family, advice and support from health professionals, accommodation, going back to work and so on.

If you are unsure, it is better to start with breastfeeding rather than to try bottle-feeding and then change your mind. The decision not to breastfeed is very hard to reverse.

Support from health professionals is essential, as breastfeeding is not necessarily instinctive. Many new mothers rely on midwives and health visitors to help them establish and continue with breastfeeding. But health professionals often work in an environment of sponsorship, promotion and 'education' from the producers of artificial baby milk (formula), and this has a strong influence on whether or not babies are breastfed.

Why breast is best

Putting aside other considerations, and looking only at the health of your baby, breastfeeding is the best option. Formula is not as good for your baby's health. Yet despite this, of the 65 per cent of women who breastfeed their babies at birth only 40 per cent continue to six weeks and even fewer to twelve weeks.

Breastmilk is the perfect food for a newborn baby because it contains everything needed for healthy growth and development during the first four months of life. The health benefits of breastfeeding can last right into adulthood, and a unique bond is forged between mother and baby.

DEFENCE AGAINST INFECTION

Breastmilk also contains antibodies that give your baby defence against infections and help fight colds, coughs, otitis media (glue ear) and stomach upsets. The protection afforded by these antibodies, especially against stomach upsets and respiratory disease, continues even after breastfeeding has ceased. Formula does not contain antibodies. Bottle-fed babies are also at greater risk of eczema, asthma, colic, constipation and ear infections and they may be at increased risk of insulin-independent diabetes. The exact mechanisms which cause eczema and asthma are still not known. It is possible that bottle-fed babies may be at greater risk because of 'missing ingredients' that would be found in breastmilk. Whatever the reason, the fact remains that they are more susceptible.

Breastmilk itself is always fresh and bacteriologically safe. Another way in which it helps prevent infection is through one of its constituents, lactoferrin, a protein that binds iron. Harmful bacteria need a good supply of iron to enable them to grow in the infant's gut; lactoferrin prevents bacteria getting that iron. Beneficial bacteria that are needed to colonise a healthy gut do not need iron.

The value of antibodies

Bacteria come in two varieties: beneficial and harmful. Antibodies are able to bind foreign substances such as viruses and damaging bacteria to help the body get rid of them. One of the most important antibodies in human milk is called secretory immunoglobulin A, or sIgA for short. It is resistant to being broken down by digestive enzymes and sticks to the gut wall, where it gives protection where it is most needed. This is because at birth there are no beneficial bacteria in a baby's gut, so it needs protection against potentially harmful bacteria which might otherwise cause diarrhoea. sIgA will carry antibodies against bacteria in the mother to which the baby will be first exposed. Throughout the time that breastfeeding is maintained sIgA will help control the way in which bacteria colonise the baby's gut.

BETTER ABSORPTION OF NUTRIENTS

Even though cow's milk contains more calcium that breastmilk, calcium is better absorbed by babies from human milk than from formula. Researchers are carrying out studies into whether formula-fed babies have weaker bones later in life.

Special enzymes in breastmilk also make a breastfed baby more efficient at digesting fats (50 per cent of the energy/calories in breastmilk is in the form of fat). The fats in human milk are far less saturated than in cow's milk. Breastmilk also contains more essential fatty acids, which are needed for the rapid growth of the baby's brain, central nervous system and immune system. It is possibly the essential fatty acids called docosahexaenoic fatty acid (DHA) and arachidonic acid found in breastmilk that contribute to breastfed babies having higher IQs than bottle-fed babies. It also makes breastmilk particularly important for premature babies.

PROTECTION FROM ALLERGIES

Breastfeeding also offers the best protection against allergic diseases such as asthma, eczema and rhinitis (runny nose linked to allergy). That is why it is especially important for babies born to atopic families (those with a history of allergy) to be exclusively breastfed for at least three months. However, this does not mean that breastfed babies will not develop allergies or related problems such as eczema, which is also influenced by early introduction of solids. In atopic families in particular there may be benefits in nursing mothers avoiding certain foods known to provoke allergies, such as dairy products. However, nursing mothers need calories and calcium, so a change of diet when breastfeeding really needs a dietitian's help.

Breastfeeding may also help prevent allergy to cow's milk in susceptible babies. One theory is that the special sIgA antibodies in breastmilk which line the inner surface of the gut prevent potentially allergenic cow's milk proteins from crossing the gut.

Other common allergens in a nursing mother's diet include chocolate, wheat, eggs, fish and oranges. If these foods provoke a reaction such as eczema in your baby, avoiding them in your diet usually solves the problem.

OPTIMUM EARLY DEVELOPMENT FOR YOUR BABY

The special bond developed when breastfeeding helps a baby thrive and the close attention, contact and 'chat' with the mother helps brain development. There are also hormones and growth factors in breastmilk that ensure the best development of your baby's brain, eyes, nervous system, intestine and internal organs during the early months of life. And although your developing baby does not receive much vitamin E or beta-carotene while in the uterus, colostrum and breastmilk during the first four to six days' production contains high levels of both to bring the baby's level up to the mother's.

CONVENIENCE

Breastmilk is easily digested, and breastfed babies do not usually become constipated. It is also the ultimate convenience food. A hungry, crying baby can be satisfied at once when breastfeeding – there is no waiting around for bottles to be sterilised, for formula to be made up and cooled or heated to the right temperature.

EASIER WEANING

Breastfeeding may also make weaning easier, as flavours from the mother's own food are thought to be experienced by the baby. The theory is that these flavours are then more acceptable during weaning because they are already familiar.

LONG-TERM BENEFITS

The long-term health benefits of breastfeeding are also thought to include lower incidence of coeliac disease, Crohn's disease and insulin-dependent diabetes.

Whether human milk protects a baby against coronary heart disease in adult life, or places him or her at greater risk of such disease, is not known. However, if the mother's diet before and during pregnancy is inadequate this may increase the baby's risk of heart disease as an adult.

ADVANTAGES FOR MOTHERS

There are advantages in breastfeeding for mothers too, including more efficient weight loss: the extra fat stored during pregnancy is used as energy to produce breastmilk. Mothers who breastfeed are also at a reduced risk of developing breast cancer and ovarian cancer. Breast-feeding ammenorrhea (loss of periods) helps with the spacing of pregnancies, with attendant health benefits for mother and babies both present and future. But it's not a reliable method of contraception.

Finally, breastfeeding saves money – formula costs around £350 in the first year.

Vitamin K at birth

The role of vitamin K is not entirely clear, but it is certainly involved in the blood-clotting process. Deficiency results in bleeding and haemorrhage, mainly in the first few months of life. The richest source in the diet is green leafy vegetables, and significant amounts are also found in other vegetables, fruit, milk and milk products, vegetable oils, meat and cereals. The safe intake set for infants by the COMA DRV Panel (1991) is 10mcg a day (about 2mcg per kilogram body weight).

Without a dose of vitamin K at birth nearly 2 per cent of babies would suffer life-threatening early haemorrhagic disease during the first week of life, and up to 10 per cent of exclusively breastfed infants would suffer late haemorrhagic disease during their first three months. Until 1990 it was standard practice to inject vitamin K into all newborns in the UK. But in that year a major study suggested that babies given vitamin K jabs at birth were twice as likely to get leukaemia or cancer than babies given an oral dose or no vitamin K. As a result, in 1992 the British Paediatric Association recommended that newborns should receive vitamin K orally, but by 1993 there had been five deaths from late haemorrhagic disease.

Since oral vitamin K obviously did not offer such prolonged protection it was decided to re-examine the effects of injections. Re-evaluation of previous studies and new studies failed to support the original links between vitamin K injections and increased risk of leukaemia and cancer. Doctors now conclude that haemorrhagic disease of the newborn can be completely eradicated without the threat of leukaemia and childhood cancer as a side-effect by giving vitamin K, but there is controversy over whether doses given may be too high.

Breastfeeding: getting started

Breastmilk is produced in response to your baby sucking at the breast. Soon after your baby is delivered, the midwife should help you put your baby to the breast.

HOW BREASTMILK ADAPTS TO
CHANGING NEEDS

The nutritional content of breastmilk varies during a feed, during the day and during the months of breastfeeding. Formula milk is always the same, and cannot be so subtly responsive to a baby's needs. In particular, the fatty acid composition of human milk changes during lactation to suit the differing requirements of each phase of your new baby's brain development. Neither can formula contain more water and less fat in hot weather, as breastmilk does.

Breastfeeding during the first few days of life is important, because the milk contains high levels of colostrum which is rich in antibodies (see page 32). This is crucial for your baby, who is now exposed for the first time to bacteria in a new environment, outside the protection of the uterus.

During the first few weeks of life babies feed frequently both by day and at night. Breastfeeding is the quickest and easiest way to respond to the frequent demands of a newborn. The more your baby feeds the more milk is produced – so the infant will not go hungry.

SUPPORT FROM OTHERS

Support from partners, family, friends and health professionals is vital when coping with the early demands of a new baby. With continued support, a routine will gradually be established. Although everyone probably wants to hold the baby, wind the baby, carry the baby, rock the baby – possibly even change the baby – practical help with routine household tasks such as shopping, cooking and washing are far more helpful. This kind of assistance will enable you to get the rest you need and concentrate on breastfeeding and caring for your new baby.

Breastfeeding does not always get off to a smooth start. Do not be afraid to ask for help from midwives and health visitors or counsellors from organisations such as the National Childbirth Trust or La Leche League (see Useful Addresses). Good support can make all the difference, and give you and your baby the time and

help you need to become expert at it. Persistence, even for a few weeks, will give your child a healthier start in life.

BREASTFEEDING OUTSIDE THE HOME

At first mothers can feel embarrassed about breastfeeding in front of others people. If you feel awkward, ask for somewhere private where you can feed your baby. As your confidence grows, if it is appropriate you will be happy to feed discreetly in front of others – with practice, and the right clothes, it can be done.

Be prepared for opposition to breastfeeding in public

As *Debrett's New Guide to Modern Etiquette* puts it:

'It is bad manners to expel any liquid from any orifice in public, and breast-feeding is no different. Nevertheless, this habit remains a very sensitive area.

The fact that this practice has not become widespread is largely due to the fact that many onlookers find the sight embarrassing, even revolting. With this in mind, well-mannered mothers should breast-feed in private. Thoughtful hosts offer lactating visitors a quiet room where they can feed away from the general throng.'

How breastfeeding works

Breasts produce milk in response to your baby feeding. So if you let your baby feed on demand you should produce the amount of milk that he or she needs. To do so you need to look after yourself: get plenty of rest, try to avoid stress, eat regularly and well, and drink plenty of water.

THE ABC OF HEALTHY EATING FOR BABIES AND TODDLERS

THE LET-DOWN REFLEX

In response to the baby's sucking, milk is 'let down' and gathers behind the nipple. The let-down reflex can happen in response to your baby's cry, so that milk leaks from your breasts.

Without the let-down reflex your baby cannot get the milk. For the reflex to happen the baby needs to feed with a wide-open mouth, taking in not only the nipple but also the area surrounding it, known as the areola. This position allows the baby's gums and lips to press against the areola, behind which the milk is stored. If the baby sucks only on the nipple he or she will not get enough milk. Stress, worry, the pain of sore nipples, and embarrassment can all stop the let-down reflex from working. If any of these problems occur seek help from your GP, midwife, health visitor or a breastfeeding counsellor or support group from one of the organisations listed on page 207.

SELECTING THE RIGHT POSITION

Putting your baby in the right position will allow him or her to take in a large mouthful of nipple and areola. Find a position in which you can hold your baby close to your breast without strain for the duration of a feed, which can be half an hour on each breast for a new baby or ten minutes for a three month baby, although frequency and duration vary enormously. This can be in a chair, sitting up in bed or lying down on your side. Whatever position you choose, your baby needs to be turned so that his or her chest is towards you. Touching the baby's cheek with the nipple will encourage him or her to 'latch on'. Make sure your baby latches on with a wide-open mouth, taking in more of the area below the nipple than above. To detach your baby from the breast, place your finger gently in the corner of your baby's mouth.

ESTABLISHING A PATTERN

During the early weeks there will probably be no particular pattern to your baby's feeds: they may be short, long, close together or far

apart. Feed when your baby needs it. Gradually a pattern will emerge, with some babies being quick feeders and others slow.

Once your baby is feeding, allow the process to continue until the infant wants to stop. You can offer the other breast straightaway i.e. before 10 minutes or after a pause, in case the baby wants more. Do not swap too quickly, or your baby may only get 'foremilk' from each breast. It is only the 'hindmilk', which comes later, which contains the calories that your baby needs. Start each feed on alternate breasts.

At first you will probably do little more than feed and change your baby, but gradually the demands will lessen and a pattern will be established. Try not to feel stressed or let things get on top of you. In just a few months, or even weeks, you will have more time for yourself and for other tasks.

YOUR BABY'S WEIGHT GAIN

Many mothers worry about whether their baby is getting enough breastmilk – you cannot tell how much your baby has consumed in the way that you can with made-up formula from a bottle. Weight gain is often slower in breastfed babies and it can be unpredictable, with less being gained in some weeks than in others. This can be a problem, as baby clinics put so much emphasis on meeting the expectations of weight gain charts. But if your baby is generally gaining weight, is healthy and has at least six really wet nappies a day (and is having nothing but breastmilk), all should be well. If, however, during the first three months your baby feeds less than five to six times in twenty-four hours, gains weight only slowly, feeds poorly or is very sleepy, consult your family doctor, health visitor or midwife.

Tips for successful breastfeeding

1. Eat a well balanced diet – and eat enough. While you are breastfeeding you need to eat well to give you energy, vitamins and minerals to cope with the round-the-clock demands of a new baby. Eating and drinking too little, or existing on a poor diet, will reduce the quantity of breastmilk. During this period be guided by your hunger. Much of the time you will feel ravenous, but when you are over-tired it is easy not to eat well. So try to eat something, even if you are very tired, and rest whenever possible. This is not the time to worry about weight loss and getting back into shape – although you are eating a lot, you are also using up the body fat stored during pregnancy to cope with demands of breastfeeding.

Stage of breastfeeding	Additional calories per day	
Up to one month	450	
Up to two months	530	
Two to three months	570	
	*	**
Three to six months	480	570
More than six months	240	550

*   Mothers whose breastmilk supplies all or most of their baby's food for the first three months
**   Mothers whose breastmilk supplies all or nearly all of the baby's food for six months or more

You will also need to drink plenty. However, avoid alcohol as it passes to your baby via breastmilk.

You will produce less milk towards the end of the day and at other times when you are tired and low in energy.

2.   An afternoon snack or meal followed by a rest can be very helpful if your baby is one of the many who like to feed a lot during the evening.

3.   On a day when breastfeeding is going well or you seem to have a good supply of milk, express some so that your partner or someone else can give the baby a feed. This will give you a rest – and give another person the pleasure of feeding the baby. It will also help accustom the baby to taking expressed milk from a bottle, which will be necessary when you wish, or need, to leave him or her with someone else.

4. Giving the occasional bottle of formula if you are worried that your baby is not getting enough milk from you will mean that you produce less milk. Despite this short-term solution being encouraged by some midwives and health professionals, it will only worsen the situation. Instead, seek help from a breastfeeding counsellor (see page 207).

5. Be careful with herbal products, other than those prescribed by a qualified herbalist, when breastfeeding, and do not drink too much herbal tea. The babies of two mothers who drank 2 litres/3½ pints of herbal tea daily to stimulate lactation suffered reduced brain growth, vomiting, limpness, poor feeding and sucking, lethargy, weak cry and poor growth. Once the mothers stopped drinking the tea, the babies' symptoms went away.

There have been a few other cases of babies suffering side-effects from herbal preparations in their mother's breastmilk. For example, when mothers took garlic capsules their babies fed for a shorter time, but there is no evidence that they took less milk. The baby of one mother using a camomile cream for sore nipples developed contact dermatitis due to the camomile. A mother who took ginseng throughout pregnancy and during breastfeeding (for irritability and mood swings) had a baby boy who was very hairy with swollen red nipples. After she stopped breastfeeding the hairiness went away. Side-effects of the ginseng, transmitted both in the uterus and from breastfeeding, were assumed to be the cause.

Fair play for mothers and babies?

The International Code of Marketing of Breastmilk Substitutes aims to protect all mothers and babies from aggressive company practices and to ensure that they receive accurate information. It bans all promotion of baby milks and other breastmilk substitutes. Baby food manufacturers may not:
- Give free supplies of artificial baby milk to hospitals
- Promote their products to the public or health workers
- Use baby pictures on their baby milk labels

- Give gifts to mothers or health workers
- Give free samples to mothers
- Promote baby foods or drinks for babies under four to six months old

But Baby Milk Action, an independent non-profit-making organisation which raises awareness of the dangers of formula and bottle feeding and campaigns to protect infant health, does not think that the baby food companies stick to the code. This is what they say:

> Most baby food manufacturers are continuing their aggressive promotion whilst claiming to abide by the International Code. They are increasingly 'investing' in health workers and health care systems, spending more money promoting their products than most governments spend on health education.
>
> Companies know that if they persuade a health worker to recommend their milk, they have gained a lifetime's brand loyalty. This is much more cost-effective than persuading mothers individually. Advertising in hospitals implies that the product is endorsed by the health service: coupled with misinformation this has created the false impression amongst mothers and health workers that many women cannot breastfeed.
>
> Even more effective is the practice of giving free or subsidised supplies of baby milk to hospitals and maternity wards. Companies claim that this is charity, but they know it makes breastfeeding more likely to fail.

The Baby Milk Action boycott of Nestlé, the largest baby food company in the world, continues, because it claims that Nestlé is perpetuating irresponsible marketing practices. The first boycott lasted from 1977 to 1984 when Nestlé agreed to abide by the code. However Baby Milk Action considered breaches were continuing and reintroduced the current boycott in 1988.

Although promotion is in theory restricted, formula manufacturers spend £6.25 on advertising per new baby compared with a budget for breastfeeding from the UK government of 9–16p per new baby (Baby Milk Action).

Bottle-feeding

Possibly because many mothers lack the right professional support, or backing from their family, friends and partners, 40 per cent of babies are bottle-fed by six weeks.

If, after considering the disadvantages of formula and bottle-feeding, you need to change from breast to bottle, do it gradually. Change first one feed a day, then two and so on.

It may help reduce the upset to your baby if someone else gives the first bottle feeds. If your baby smells you, he or she will smell and therefore expect breastmilk and will not take happily to a bottle. Even if you need or want to change to bottle-feeding consider retaining one or more feeds, perhaps early morning or bedtime, for breastfeeding. The amount of milk you produce will adjust to suit the demands.

However, if your circumstances change so that you can resume breastfeeding it is possible to do so (even women who have not recently had a baby, but who have previously fully breast fed for at least two weeks, can relactate). Success depends on how frequently you put the baby to the breast to stimulate lactation.

WHAT IS FORMULA?

Most formula, or artificial baby milk, is based on cow's milk, which is the perfect food for calves. For human babies it contains too much protein, sodium and minerals, too little sugar and the wrong kind of fat. Manufacturers make varying degrees of effort to adapt the composition of cow's milk products to resemble human milk, but formula cannot offer the immunological protection of breastmilk. Even if antibodies from cow's milk were present in formula they would not be helpful to babies, because they are designed to protect against micro-organisms likely to cause disease in cattle.

Attempts by genetic engineers to get cows to produce human lactoferrin in their milk, for use in manufacture of formula, continue. Cows could also be immunised with infectious agents so that they produce high levels of antibodies similar to those in human colostrum. The antibodies could be purified and added to infant formula. But manipulation of cow's milk-based formula to produce biologically active humanised baby milk seems a long way off. In the meantime, breast remains best for immunological protection.

Formula based on soya is also made for babies and used in situations where it is felt that normal formula would cause problems. Standard soya milk should not be substituted for soya formula because, like cow's milk, it does not contain the proper ratio or type of protein, fat and carbohydrates, nor the vitamins and minerals needed for use as a sole food.

Recent concern about phytoestrogens (plant hormones) in soya formula (see page 176) has prompted advice from the Department of Health not to use soya formula unless advised to do so by a doctor, midwife or health visitor because of allergy to cow's milk or intolerance to lactose (milk sugar in formula). Soya formula is also potentially more damaging to babies' teeth as the lactose (milk sugar) is replaced by other sugars such as glucose, sucrose and maltose which have greater potential to cause dental decay. Some parents believe that soya formula is less likely to result in their infants having allergies, but studies have not consistently proved this.

Special formulas from which the allergenic proteins of cow's milk have been removed are also available on the recommendation of a doctor or dietitian. However, they need to be introduced very early because they have unpleasant flavours and older babies will reject them.

CONSTIPATION

Formula-fed babies are more likely than breastfed ones to become constipated. This can occur if the formula is made up incorrectly, especially if too much powder is added to the water. Small drinks of cooled boiled water may help. Discuss the problem with your GP or health visitor.

FEEDING EQUIPMENT

You need to be well organised for bottle feeding so that you do not keep a hungry baby waiting. If not, no one will enjoy feed time.

BOTTLES AND TEATS

At least six bottles and teats are needed. If you use secondhand bottles, check that they are not too scratched; if they are, you will not be able to sterilise them properly. Always use new teats, which come in all sorts of shapes and with different hole sizes. If the hole is too small your baby will have to suck too hard and too long to obtain enough milk. If it is too big your baby will probably spit and splutter as the milk comes through too quickly. You may need to experiment to find the right size, so only buy one at a time until you are sure.

OTHER EQUIPMENT

You will need a bottle brush, and salt to clean teats.

TYPES OF STERILISING EQUIPMENT

Before sterilising wash the bottles and teats thoroughly in washing up liquid. Use a bottle brush to get rid of every trace of milk, and squirt water through the teats. Rubbing salt inside teats before washing helps remove milk. Rinse in clean water.

USING A CHEMICAL STERILISER

Chemical sterilising units are available, or you can use a plastic bucket with a lid.

Immerse washed bottles and teats (including the brush) in the sterilising solution. Agitate the bottles to make sure there are no air bubbles in them and leave in the solution for the time given in the instructions on the pack of sterilising solution/tablets. Make up a quantity of sterilising solution from tablets or liquid as instructed on the pack.

If you are using a bucket, keep everything under the water by putting a plate on top.

If you want to rinse the bottles afterwards to remove traces of sterilising solution, use boiled cooled water – tap water will make them unsterile again.

STERILISING BY BOILING

Wash the bottles and teats as described above. Put them in a large pan with a lid, and agitate to remove air bubbles. Put on the lid and boil for at least ten minutes. Leave in the covered pan until needed.

STEAM STERILISERS

Electric units to steam-sterilise bottles and teats avoid the need for chemicals. These free-standing units plug into a standard socket. Bottles and teats are washed as above, then placed in the machine. A small quantity of water is added and the machine turned on. The contents are sterilised within ten minutes. (This is only a guide to the way the process works – always follow the manufacturer's instructions carefully.)

MICROWAVE STERILISERS

These units fit into a microwave oven. Bottles and teats are washed as above, then placed in the unit. A small quantity of water is added to the unit, which is then placed in the oven for the length of time indicated in the manufacturer's instructions. (Again, this is only a guide to the way the process works – follow the manufacturer's instructions carefully.)

WHICH FORMULA TO CHOOSE

Before giving your baby formula, talk to your doctor, health visitor or midwife, or to a breastfeeding counsellor. Decide whether to use one based on cow's milk or soya. Discuss special needs such as anti-allergy products with your GP or health visitor.

Cow's milk formula can be either whey-based or casein-based. Whey is the clear liquid left after milk protein has been clotted and most of the fat removed, for instance after cheese-making. Whey-based formulas are usually given to new babies as the ratio of casein to whey is closer to that of breastmilk, and whey is supposed to be easier to digest.

Casein-based formula contains more protein and minerals and is absorbed more slowly. Often these formulas are recommended for 'hungrier' babies. They should not normally be used before six months.

Soya formula is based on soya protein. As it is often used for babies who cannot tolerate lactose (milk sugar) it contains non-milk sugars, which are potentially more harmful to teeth.

The main formulas available are shown in the table.

Whey	Casein	Follow-on
SMA Gold	SMA White	SMA Progress
Cow & Gate Premium	Cow & Gate Plus	Cow & Gate Step-Up
Farley's First Milk	Farley's Second Milk	Farley's Follow-on Milk
Milupa Aptamil	Milupa Milumil	Follow-up Forward
Boots Infant Milk Formula 1	Boots Infant Milk Formula 2	Boots Follow-on Milk
Sainsbury's First Menu first stage milk	Sainsbury's Second Menu second stage milk	Sainsbury's Follow-on Milk

There are other special formulas for premature babies, and your doctor, midwife, dietitian or health visitor will advise you on these if necessary.

No formula milks contain the living maternal cells that give babies the immunological benefits of breastmilk, nor the enzymes, hormones and other specific active factors. Some contain added ingredients which attempt to mimic substances naturally present in breastmilk. Manufacturers are not allowed to make claims for these on the packs; however, they do promote them to health workers, claiming that their formulas are 'enriched' to match breastmilk. On the pack they can only claim 'adapted protein' 'low sodium', 'sucrose-free', 'lactose only', 'lactose-free' and 'iron-enriched'.

LONG CHAIN FATTY ACIDS

LCPs are designed to mimic the long chain fatty acids found in breastmilk, called arachidonic acid and docosahexaenoic acid

(DHA). As explained earlier, LCPs are essential for the proper development of the brain and nervous system, and may contribute to breastfed babies having higher IQs, better eyesight and fewer brain dysfunctions causing movement abnormalities than formula-fed babies. Despite encouragement from the World Health Organisation since the late 1970s, it was only in 1993 that LCPs were introduced to just one brand of formula on sale in Britain (apart from special formula for premature babies), and this cost parents an extra £12 or so for three months' supply. Other brands now contain added LCPs. However, these LCPs do not make formula as good as breastmilk.

Learning ability in babies has been shown to be best at three months in breastfed babies, second-best in those fed formula with LCPs, and least good in babies on standard formula, who show poor control of their attention and respond less well to stimulus. At nine to ten months the same differences are apparent, with breastfed babies examining new toys in the most controlled way and learning how to use them more quickly than other infants. Follow-up studies at the age of nine also confirm that breastfed babies perform best.

While doctors are concerned that formula milk may not contain enough DHA for brain development, there is also concern about the type of polyunsaturated fatty acids being added to formula to mimic DHA. To obtain LCPs manufacturers of artificial baby milk use various sources such as eggs, fish oil, blackcurrant seed oil, algae, genetically engineered yeasts and other biotechnology sources.

Even if the LCPs added to formula are beneficial, there may be problems with using sources that are not normally part of the diet of new babies – or even of older babies. Some of the sources may provoke allergies and food intolerance; not all have been fully tested. At the moment UK food regulations do not require manufacturers to seek approval before adding LCPs to artificial baby milk. Nor is there a legal requirement for scientific and clinical assessment before marketing baby milk with added fatty acids.

Some of the claims for LCPs in formula that were initially printed on containers have been dropped, following complaints to trading standards authorities. However, if long chain fatty acids are considered so essential for brain development then we may be prepared to get them from many different sources. Parents will have to weigh up for themselves the benefit against the possible problems caused by the source.

Other substances that the EU has recently considered safe for addition to infant formula include the mineral selenium; nucleotides, which are partially broken down (digested) proteins; and carnitine, a fat-burning substance produced naturally in the muscles from the amino acid (protein) lysine. The theory is that nucleotides will improve protein absorption and gut function (demonstrated in animals), and carnitine will make up for the lack of lipase, a natural enzyme found in breastmilk that helps babies digest fat and fat-soluble vitamins (breastmilk is 50–60 per cent fat).

It will astonish parents that none of these theories has been proved, as critics of formula, including eminent professors of child health and nutrition, point out. In an attempt to get formula manufacturers to improve their products they recommend that such modifications to formula should be assessed nutritionally in the light of outcomes of healthy babies exclusively breastfed for four to six months. They also want formula to be tested for safety and efficacy – not a lot to ask!

CONTAMINANTS IN ARTIFICIAL BABY MILK

The risks from contaminants such as heavy metals, phthalates, lindane, phytoestrogens and non-milk sugars (see Chapter 5) may be long-term and difficult or even impossible to measure. There are also risks of allergy from added ingredients that would not be found in breastmilk, such as egg, peanut oil (which has now been removed from formula), genetically engineered material and other substances that should not be given to young babies (again, see Chapter 5). New EU controls on maximum levels of contaminants in baby milk do not come into force until March 1999.

MAKING UP FEEDS

1. Always use fresh water.
2. Do not reboil water, as this evaporates some of it and concentrates the mineral salts.

3. Do not use artificially softened water as it may contain high levels of sodium. If your tap water contains high levels of lead, consider buying a water filter that can remove heavy metal contamination. Low dose exposure to lead may result in a decrease in IQ. (Lead can also find its way into breastmilk, so nursing mothers too might want to invest in a water filter, or to drink bottled mineral water). If you are using bottled water, always use still rather than carbonated and boil it and cool it as for tap water. Check the label to ensure that it contains less than 25mg sodium per 100ml.

4. Follow the instructions on the pack and dilute the exact amount of powder as directed. Do not add any extra powder, sugar, cereal or anything else – there is a risk that your baby could become dehydrated if the feed is too concentrated, or could choke on solids added to a bottle. Formula has been produced carefully to give your baby the calories and nutrients it needs without anything else being added. Follow-on (that is, higher calorie) formula is available for older and/or hungrier babies over six months. Making a feed too weak may mean that your baby will not get enough calories. As a guide, a baby needs about 150ml milk per 1kg of body weight every twenty-four hours (2½ oz per lb).

TIME-SAVING TIP

Making up a day's feeds and storing them in the fridge in capped bottles saves time and means that you will not have to make your baby wait while you make up a feed. Shake the bottle well before use, and do not store made-up milk for more than twenty-four hours.

FEEDING

Bottles can be warmed before a feed by standing them in either a jug or an insulated container of hot water, or an electric bottle warmer (a free-standing unit with a plug). Test the temperature by shaking some milk from the bottle on to the inside of your wrist. Throw away warm milk after one hour and do not reheat it; warm milk is a breeding ground for bacteria. Do not warm milk in a microwave

oven, because it continues to heat up after it has been taken from the oven. The bottle may feel cool, but the milk inside may be too hot and you would risk seriously scalding your baby.

Some babies are quite happy with cold milk straight from the fridge. If this is the case, it will speed up preparation for feed times.

If your baby is thirsty in hot weather, offer water. Use boiled, cooled water and sterilise the bottle and teat as for a milk feed (see page 46).

FEEDING TIP

Keep the bottle tilted so that the teat is full of milk. If air gets in, the baby may take in too much air and suffer wind or colic (see below). Never prop up a bottle and leave a baby alone with it – the infant could choke.

COLIC

Babies with colic scream as if in pain and go red in the face. When you feel the child's tummy it is hard and tense. Colic usually comes on within an hour of a feed, can last for hours, and is more common during the evening. The crying is very distressing for parents because, no matter what you do, your baby is unable to settle; if the child does go off to sleep it may only be a short while before he or she wakes and cries again. The only consolation is that the condition is often referred to as 'three-month colic' because it usually disappears after that time.

No one really knows what causes colic, but it is probably abdominal pain brought on by wind. A distended abdomen may be caused by babies taking in too much air when they feed, which is why bottlefed babies are more commonly affected than breastfed ones. Other theories are that colic could be due to the unbalanced bacteria content of the baby's immature digestive system or a reaction to cow's milk, either as a component of formula or as a reaction to it in the nursing mother's diet.

Despite the awful crying, colic will not harm your baby. And if your baby is contented during the rest of the day then it almost certainly is colic. However, if you are worried, or if your baby goes pale or limp or develops vomiting and diarrhoea, see your doctor at once as it might be something more serious.

COPING WITH COLIC

Try to find someone to look after your baby for a few hours if you are desperate for sleep. This could be during the day so that you are less tired when the evening bout of colic occurs. If you cannot find help put your baby in the cot, shut the door and have a few minutes away from the crying (which won't hurt the child).

Wind your baby halfway through a feed as well as at the end. Some babies are helped by an anti-spasmodic preparation such as Infacol (available from the chemist) which is given before feeds. If you are really desperate contact an organisation called CRY-SIS for support (see page 208 for telephone number).

DIARRHOEA

This condition is dangerous in babies because they can dehydrate quickly, especially if they are vomiting as well. Usually the diarrhoea clears up within twenty-four hours, but if it does not, or your baby shows signs of dehydration – such as drowsiness, prolonged crying, unresponsiveness, glazed eyes, a depressed fontanelle and a dry, sticky mouth or tongue – call a doctor urgently.

If your baby has diarrhoea, do not give milk. Instead, give an electrolyte mixture such as Dioralyte from the chemist to replace lost water and salts. Milk can be gradually reintroduced over a twenty-four-hour period:

● First feed: one part baby milk to three parts water
● Second feed: equal parts baby milk and water
● Third feed: three parts baby milk to one part water
● Fourth feed: undiluted

Milk feeds are stopped because the diarrhoea can cause a temporary deficiency of the enzyme lactase which is needed to digest lactose (milk sugar). If you continue to feed your baby with milk it could lead to a lactose intolerance (inability to absorb milk sugar), and to more serious and prolonged diarrhoea.

DUMMIES

Soothers, pacifiers or dummies, call them what you will, generate fierce debate.

IN FAVOUR

Those in favour say that dummies satisfy a baby's need to suck and can be taken away (unlike a thumb) around five months or so, before they affect the shape of the teeth or mouth. The trouble is that most parents do not remove them before the baby has come to rely on them, and rather than use a dummy for short-term relief from a crying baby they use them at every whimper. There are even orthodontic dummies for sale which are supposed to do less harm to a baby's teeth.

AGAINST

Those against say that babies who suck dummies may turn out to be less intelligent than those allowed to cry. Dummies may make babies so soporific that they do not notice their surroundings and have less interaction with their mothers, say researchers, but then many babies given dummies go on to study to PhD level! Researchers add that babies prepared to accept a counterfeit nipple (which is what a dummy is) are less intelligent than those who refuse dummies. Refusing a dummy and continuing to cry is the behaviour which is most likely to result in interaction with parents – just what an intelligent baby wants. Peaceful babies who suck dummies are likely to attract less attention – and talk – from their parents, and so receive less stimulation.

The same study controversially reinterpreted previous feeding data which suggested that babies who are exclusively breastfed are likely to have a higher IQ than those fed breast and bottle, or bottle alone. The new interpretation suggested that in previous studies higher social class (associated today with the practice of breast feeding) had more to do with higher IQ than did the method of feeding. The new and controversial conclusion was that the baby's social environment had more to do with his or her later intelligence than did the nutritional quality of the milk. The use of a dummy in infancy (together with the number of brothers and sisters, mother's age and father's occupational class) were better predictors of adult intelligence than type of feeding.

This does not mean that using a dummy is the cause of lower intelligence (any more than formula feeding is). It is more likely to mean that parents who use dummies are ignoring advice not to do so, possibly because they are less intelligent or have weaker parenting skills.

However, in previous studies when maternal intelligence was measured directly and used to adjust differences which suggest that breastfed babies have slightly higher IQs, no real difference in intelligence between breastfed and formula-fed babies emerged. More intelligent women (irrespective of social class and education) have more intelligent babies (irrespective of breast- or bottle-feeding). Some would say that more intelligent women are likely to choose to breastfeed. Others would say that intelligent, loving and caring mothers are likely to have intelligent children, regardless of how they feed them as babies or whether they give them dummies.

Other people dislike dummies because they are unhygienic unless scrupulously cleaned and regularly replaced throughout the day. There is also an argument that babies need to learn to pacify themselves rather than rely on a parent to put a dummy back in their mouth. It is suggested that dummies may 'confuse' a baby about sucking, which should really be used for breastfeeding. There is a feeling that a dummy is used to pacify the child rather than attend to its real needs.

There is also a definite class attitude against dummies. It has been argued that upper-class people can despatch a crying child from the room with its nanny and therefore have no need for dummies, which are seen as the purview of the lower class. Many people simply do not like the look of babies with dummies. Accusations that they impair or delay speech, however, are largely unproved.

CHAPTER 3

Weaning

Your baby's diet, with menus, from four to twelve months, plus menus for toddlers from 1 to 3 years

After the first few months of life your baby's needs are no longer met entirely by breastmilk. Around the age of four months solid food is introduced. Although we talk about starting a baby on 'solids' after four months, weaning foods are smooth purees not much thicker than milk. To begin with they are given in addition to breastmilk or formula, but gradually babies reduce their milk intake and eat larger amounts of food.

The aim is for your baby, by the age of one year, to be eating a well-balanced, varied diet that is more or less the same as that of the rest of the family. The baby's foods will, however, still need to be chopped.

The best encouragement for your baby to enjoy food is to eat with the rest of the family. This should also lead to acceptance of a wide range of food through imitation (making it important for the rest of the family also to eat a well-balanced and varied diet!). After all, food is more fun when shared, and always eating by yourself in the high chair must be a lonely experience.

However, it is important to realise early on that what constitutes a healthy diet for an adult is not a healthy diet for a baby or toddler. The high fibre, low fat diet that is best for adults should not be given

56

THE ABC OF HEALTHY EATING FOR BABIES AND TODDLERS

to infants and young children under five years old, who may not be able to obtain from it enough calories, vitamins and minerals to ensure their proper mental and physical development.

Weaning summary

At all stages salt or sugar should not be added to your baby's food.

STAGE 1: FOUR TO SIX MONTHS

Your baby continues to get most of his or her nutrition from breastmilk while learning to take pureed food from a spoon such as fruit and vegetables, baby rice, mashed potato, soft cooked meat and pulses, yogurt and fromage frais.

STAGE 2: SIX TO NINE MONTHS
TRANSITIONAL

A wider variety of food and different textures are introduced, including meat, fish, eggs and cereals. Finger foods can be introduced, and wheat and cow's milk (in cooking and to mix solids) can be given.

STAGE 3: NINE MONTHS TO A YEAR

Your baby should be enjoying three meals a day, with snacks and/or drinks between meals. Some foods can be normal adult texture, others chopped and mashed

Weaning step by step

Try to take a relaxed attitude to weaning (easily said, as it can be a tense time) and be guided by your baby. If solids are at first refused, leave it a few days before trying again – but don't leave it too long as babies are most receptive to new tastes up to the age of six months.

It may be tempting to try to persuade your baby to eat more, especially if you are a first-time mother whose measure of progress is your baby's growth and weight gain charts, but try to be guided by your baby's appetite. Look out for the child's cues that indicate hunger or fullness, and use them to avoid overfeeding or underfeeding. This will also help your baby learn to follow his or her own internal signals of hunger and fullness.

Home-made or bought baby foods?

Most parents use a combination of both.

COMMERCIALLY PREPARED BABY FOODS

- Can be quicker and more convenient, especially for working mothers and when travelling
- Guarantee hygiene in preparation
- Guarantee certain nutritional standards (but they may not be what you would expect)

These foods are obviously popular as UK sales are worth more than £120 million a year and 80 per cent of Britain's 1 million babies aged between four and twenty months eat them. Yet when you compare the natural-sounding names such as Spring Vegetable Dinner or Apricot Custard with the actual ingredients listed in the small print, you soon realise that you have to choose carefully. Many commercially prepared baby foods may be watery mixtures padded out with starches such as modified cornflour, thickeners such as rice flour and soya flour, and sugar – especially baby puddings and drinks. Even the baby foods boasting they are 'healthy' and containing no artificial flavourings, no artificial colouring, no artificial sweeteners, no added salt and no added sugar need careful scrutiny of their ingredients.

For example, many meat meals contain as little as 10 per cent meat, and much of that is not the lean meat you would imagine it to be. When current EU proposals become law, Britain's baby food manufacturers will be forced to include a minimum of 40 per cent meat by weight, but even that is not much in a meat-based meal. Even worse, 'mainly meat' meals could contain only 10 per cent meat, and 'meat with' meals 8 per cent. And this is an improvement! At the moment the protein content is boosted by cheap substitutes such as soya protein; the flavour is enhanced by hydrolysed vegetable protein; vitamins and minerals are added to make up for the lack of nutritious real food ingredients or over-processed food such as dried packet baby food. Tomato puree is used to give colour and flavour to what would otherwise be a watery mixture. In addition, dried baby food and 'fruit puddings' will be limited to 20 per cent sugar, and desserts to (a massive) 25 per cent sugar! No wonder there is a rise in tooth decay among under-fives in Britain.

While certain additives (some preservatives, artificial sweeteners and artificial colours) are not permitted in foods sold specifically for babies and toddlers, other foods that contain them are craftily targeted at children. For example some brands of fromage frais contain for too much sugar, colouring, preservatives, thickeners, starches and other unnecessary additives that build profits for manufacturers but do not contribute to building healthy bodies for babies.

All this is not meant to make working mothers who consider they have no choice but to leave formula or jars, packets and cans of baby food with the childminder feel guilty. It is by way of ensuring that, when buying baby food, you are an informed consumer. For more guidelines on choosing wisely see page 61.

HOME-MADE FOOD

● Can be more economical
● Allows complete control over ingredients and therefore what baby eats
● Offers a wider range of foods, which is important in establishing a varied healthy diet for childhood – and life
● Avoids unnecessary non-nutritional cheap fillers and additives (although many are not permitted in baby food)

As babies turn into toddlers they will derive a lot of fun from 'helping' prepare food and cooking – this is something that you can enjoy together. Of course, commercial baby food companies express this differently. They say their foods are a great help because they save you time which can then be spent with your baby! Doing what?

Some studies suggest that certain home-made baby foods may be low in iron and zinc and contain more salt than manufactured foods. On the other hand, some commercial baby food is less nutritious and certainly does not taste like 'real' food, which is what you are aiming to give your baby a taste for.

Whether you opt entirely for home-prepared foods in the belief that they are nutritionally superior (see recipes in Chapter 4), or for commercially prepared foods for whatever reason, you still have to balance your baby's diet well. **This is what the unique menus in this book do for you, as they ensure that the recommended daily servings of different food groups are met.**

Buying baby foods

To start with this will be time-consuming as you need to read the labels, especially the ingredients list, very carefully to get to know which baby foods are full of nutritious ingredients and which are padded out with cheap fillers. When you read the labels you are looking for recognisable food ingredients. Whether the food is a savoury main course or a dessert the ingredient giving its name to the dish (such as chicken for Chicken Dinner or apricots for Apricot Dessert) should be the first ingredient listed, which would indicate it is the main ingredient. Unfortunately this will hardly ever be the case because the meat and fruit content of commercial baby food is low (as it is in most adult ready-meals) to maximise profit for the manufacturer and retailer.

WHAT TO LOOK FOR WHEN BUYING BABY FOOD

1. Avoid wet baby foods (that is, jars of food) that contain water as a main ingredient (in which case it will appear as the first or second ingredient listed).

2. Avoid desserts in which sugar or water are the first listed ingredients. Sugar can also appear on labels disguised as: glucose, glucose syrup, fructose, concentrated fruit juice, sucrose, dextrose, honey, invert sugar, maltose, hydrolysed starch, corn syrup.

3. Avoid baby foods that contain filler or sweetener ingredients which offer little nutritional value. Examples are skimmed milk powder, whey, caseine, maltodextrin, sugar and soya flour. These ingredients are used instead of more expensive 'real food'.

4. Be wary of fruit varieties of baby food that do not contain real fruit. Often the so-called fruit in desserts is only added juice or juice concentrate. The nutritional advantages of real fruit will not be present in these foods.

5. Although additives and artificial sweeteners are not permitted in baby foods, be wary of foods that contain vitamin-related pigments such as riboflavin and beta-carotene which are not present in large enough quantities to be nutritionally valuable, but are there to give colour to so-called fruit yogurt, fromage frais and desserts. If they had enough fruit in them to give natural colour they would not need these 'natural' colourings.

6. Check out the sugar content on the nutritional panel on the label. Sugar comes under carbohydrates. Sometimes it is listed separately, at other times it is 'hidden' as carbohydrate so that you will have to guesstimate how much is in the food. Nutritional breakdowns are given per 100 grams or per Xg portion. One teaspoon of sugar equals 5g.

7. Be suspicious of long ingredients lists which often reveal lots of fillers and few 'real food' ingredients. As a rule of thumb, the shorter the list the better (except, perhaps, for a mixed grain baby muesli).

8. Avoid jars of baby yogurt dessert where yogurt is way down the ingredients list and water is nearer the top. It is cheaper and more nutritious to buy a natural (organic) yogurt and stir in fruit (fresh or dried) puree, or pieces of fruit for older babies.

9. Avoid getting your older baby/toddler into the habit of unnecessary snacks as everyday food. Limit to parties and occasional treats teddy bear crisps, biscuits, animal-shaped crackers and herbal drinks (mainly maltodextrin or skimmed milk powder with added herb/fruit flavour).

10. If you buy rusks or 'teething biscuits', opt for Bickiepeg teething biscuits for babies because they have no added sugar or salt.

N.B. When labels say Stage 1 foods they are for babies aged four to six months. Stage 2 foods are for babies six to nine months.

DRIED BABY FOOD IN PACKETS VERSUS WET BABY FOOD IN JARS

Objectively speaking, dried and fresh (wet) baby foods are nutritionally very similar. The fortification with vitamins and minerals, for example, is controlled by food regulations and will be similar in both. However, aesthetically jars of baby food would seem to be 'fresher' and more like home-made baby foods although some have very long shelf lives, up to three years, and there is vitamin loss over time.

Criticisms of dried packet foods are that they are extremely bland and do nothing to develop a baby's taste for the flavours and textures of real food that it is hoped will form the basis of his or her diet, once weaned. Some of the dried packet savoury foods also contain added sugar and milk powder which makes them unnaturally sweet – possibly influencing a baby's tastes in the wrong direction. Dried packet foods (and some jars) for the second stage of weaning may not provide enough change in texture to develop a baby's ability to chew and come to terms with lumpier food. Of course you can always add vegetables and fruit to dried packet food, but this negates the convenience factor which is popular with many busy mums.

Because of the drawbacks of dried packet foods it would be wise not to rely on them entirely. Use a mixture of packets and jars. Better still, use home-made as well to familiarise your baby with the tastes of the family food on to which he or she will ideally be weaned.

Avoid shopping trolley tantrums

As your toddler becomes more aware and able to recognise biscuits, crisps, confectionery and sticky cakes from the bakery counter, there will be constant demands for them as you go round the supermarket. If it is a habit to give food as you go round the shop to 'keep them quiet', start as you mean to go on and buy a more nutritious snack that they can eat as they sit in the trolley. A sandwich, a plain bun, unsalted crisps or Twiglets would all be suitable.

WHICH BRANDS TO BUY

You will find the most nutritious and best-tasting commercial baby foods in the following ranges (in alphabetical order, not order of preference). Many manufacturers have telephone helplines, often free (see Useful Addresses on page 208).

BABY ORGANIX ORGANIC BABY FOOD

The range includes Stage I and Stage II weaning foods, both wet (jars) and dried, desserts, toddler meals (jars), pasta and pasta sauces. Vegetarian varieties are fortified to meet the nutritional needs of babies on meat-free diet. Baby Organix Baby's Yogurt (four-packs) natural or fruit (containing real fruit, not juice concentrates) can be obtained from some supermarkets. Some are sweetened with honey. The main range can be found in supermarkets, health food shops and chemists (including Boots).

BOOTS MOTHERS RECIPE ORGANIC BABY FOOD – SWEET AND SAVOURY

The range includes Stage I and Stage II weaning foods in jars and baby rice, Stage I breakfast cereal, Stage II muesli and pasta, and

toddler meals. Boots First Harvest range is not organic, but to quote Boots: 'ingredients are obtained in the most natural way e.g. man-made fertilisers avoided and traditional farming methods used, livestock humanely reared'. The range is free from peanuts and peanut oil. In addition there are sweet and savoury Stage I and Stage II weaning foods in jars, Stage II breakfast cereal, and baby juices.

COW & GATE
There is a limited range of four organic early weaning foods called Organic Choice, wet foods (jars), two fruit and two vegetable varieties.

HIPP ORGANIC BABY FOOD
The range includes Stage I and Stage II weaning foods, both wet (jars) and dried, desserts and toddler meals (jars). There are also ready-to-drink juices (bottles). All these are available from supermarkets, health food shops and chemists (including Boots).

ORIGINAL FRESH BABYFOOD
As the name suggests, these are fresh foods (similar to adult ready-meals) sold from the supermarket chiller counter. Although not organic, they are freshly prepared foods well flavoured with herbs and spices. Their adventurous flavours (like some of the Baby Organix range) should, theoretically, develop a taste for what were traditionally considered more 'grown up' flavours, so that your baby is not weaned on to a restricted, bland diet. This brand is more costly than conventional packets and jars.

ALSO RECOMMENDED
● Familia Muesli baby food (but only from the age of six months, as it contains wheat and rye)
● Milupa organic Natural Choice breakfast cereals range (but look out for added sugar, although they contain less than in the standard range)
● Supermarket own brands (but choose carefully – only a few in each range are free from added sugars and bulkers)

- Heinz Pure Fruit range of desserts is excellent. For main courses, pick and choose carefully to find some that will fit the shopping criteria (see page 61).
- Olvarit: as for Heinz
- Beech-Nut brand of baby food, imported from the US. Nutritionally a sound range of wet food in jars that relies on real food ingredients and no added sugar. Limited availability.

OCCASIONALLY USEFUL

Ready-to-drink pure fruit juices and water with a hint of fruit are expensive, but useful in an emergency when you are out and about but have forgotten to take your baby's usual drink – especially if there is a teat attached. However, for older babies they are not a good idea as they should be encouraged to drink from a beaker. Read the label carefully to ensure that these drinks contain only water, fruit juice or natural flavourings and nothing less innocuous than vitamin C.

Making Your Own Baby Food

HYGIENE

When preparing and serving baby foods be especially careful about hygiene.

1. Wash your hands thoroughly before you start, and between handling raw and cooked foods (particularly meats). This prevents salmonella or other food poisoning bacteria on raw food being transferred to other foods.

2. Sterilise all feeding equipment and bowls until your baby is six months old. (See page 46.) After six months you need only sterilise bottles and teats and drinking spouts.

EQUIPMENT

Standard kitchen equipment is suitable for home-made baby food. You will need either a sieve or a small mouli-grater or blender. A small blender is useful for preparing batches of food which can then be frozen in individual portions in ice cube trays (each ice cube provides three teaspoons or one tablespoon of food, which is all your baby will eat to start with, and small portions mean less wastage if the food is not eaten).

Begin with a tiny weaning bowl (or the sterilised plastic top from a feeding bottle such as Avent). Choose a shallow plastic spoon from which the baby can suck the food. A dish with a sucker on the base to secure it to the high chair tray may be useful later on. A dish is important, even when using baby food from a jar. Use a clean spoon to put a portion into a dish. Do not feed from the jar – if you do you will have to throw away any uneaten food, whereas untouched food in the jar can have the lid put back on and be stored for a further twenty-four hours in the fridge. You will also need a bib for your baby. Soft cotton bibs are best at first. Toddlers can have a plastic bib with a trough (sometimes called a Pelican bib). It's amazing what combinations they like eating from the trough.

BATCH 'COOKING'

If you are preparing home-made food it makes sense to do a lot and freeze some for future use. This will save time later and make it easier for you to provide food quickly to meet the demands of a hungry (which usually means crying) baby.

Cool food as quickly as possible once it is cooked (and pureed, if appropriate). Keep it covered at all times and do not leave it standing around at room temperature, either before or after pureeing: food poisoning bacteria breed quickly in warm food. Put ice cube trays of cooled food into the fridge first to reduce the temperature before freezing.

Freezer storage times

Fruit and vegetable purees	Six months
Fruit and vegetable purees with added milk/fromage frais	Two months
Fish and meat	Three months

Ideally, home-made frozen foods should be defrosted slowly in the fridge, but many parents find it convenient to defrost and reheat their baby's food in a microwave oven immediately before serving it. This is not recommended because it can result in uneven thawing and 'hot spots' in the food that could scald your baby's mouth. To prevent this risk, stir food during and after cooking, then leave it to stand before rechecking the temperature and serving. Put a small amount of food on a spoon and hold it against the inside of your wrist – as you may have previously done to test the temperature of your baby's milk.

If you use clingfilm in the microwave, choose a non-pvc variety and do not let it touch your baby's food.

Storing baby food

- Cover unused home-made food and store it in the fridge for up to twenty-four hours
- Only reheat food once
- Keep unserved purchased baby food in covered jars in the fridge for up to forty-eight hours
- Do not store food in opened cans, but transfer unserved food to a non-metallic container for storing, covered, in the fridge
- Only use clingfilm in contact with high fat foods (cheese, raw meats with fat, pastry) if the pack states that it is suitable or non-PVC
- Do not store half-eaten food – throw away what your baby does not want

First tastes

To start with, offer your baby one food at a time. Never add salt or sugar to baby food, even if it tastes bland to you. Babies have ten

thousand tastebuds (compared with two thousand in adults), so what tastes bland to us should be full of flavour to them. Sugar also risks tooth decay later on, and a baby's kidneys are too immature to cope with salt.

Fruit and vegetable purees and baby rice are excellent first foods. From four months try:

- Purees of cooked apple, pear, potato, sweet potato, parsnip, carrot, squash, broccoli, courgette, cauliflower or swede
- Avocado, banana, papaya and peaches do not need to be cooked before they are pureed
- Rice should be the first cereal you use because it does not contain gluten, a protein found in wheat, oats, barley and rye that can cause food allergy if introduced too early (before six months). Make up baby rice with expressed breastmilk, formula or cooled boiled water.

SHOPPING TIP: BABY RICE

Read ingredients panels on packs of baby rice: despite skimmed milk powder and sugar being undesirable for babies of four months, many brands of baby rice contain them. Ground rice or rice flakes from the supermarket are sugar-free and cheaper than baby rice.

Self-feeding

Give your baby a spoon to hold as soon as he or she is interested, although real attempts at self-feeding don't start until around a year old. Good finger foods, from around eight months, include:

- Slices of peeled apple, pear, banana, carrot, celery (destring, if you have the patience), or cubes of hard cheese such as Cheddar or Edam
- Lightly steamed or boiled (and cooled) carrot sticks, French beans and broccoli florets
- Teething biscuits or rusks without added sugar, such as Bickie-pegs, are enjoyed by babies, but fingers of bread, toast and crispbread are cheaper

THE ABC OF HEALTHY EATING FOR BABIES AND TODDLERS

Food allergies

Babies are most susceptible to food allergies in the first few months of life. Breastfeeding, as already explained, seems to offer some protection. However, it is safest not to give foods likely to cause allergy to babies born into families with a history of allergic disease (asthma, allergy-related eczema, allergic rhinitis, hay fever) before eight months at the earliest. Nuts can cause some of the most severe allergies, and since they need not be a major part of the diet (except perhaps for vegan babies and toddlers) their introduction can be delayed even longer. One eminent researcher suggests waiting until the age of five years for 'at risk' babies. Babies without allergy can have smooth nut butters from the age of eight months. Do not give whole or chopped nuts to children under three years old because of the risk of choking. For more information on nut allergies see page 169.

Weaning plan for 'at risk' infants

STAGE 1: BIRTH TO FOUR/SIX MONTHS

Exclusive demand breastfeeding.

STAGE 2: SIX TO EIGHT MONTHS

Root vegetables and non-citrus fruit, other vegetables and cereals (except wheat), supplementary breastfeeding.

STAGE 3: EIGHT TO TEN MONTHS

Wheat, citrus fruits, meats (beef and chicken last), supplementary breastfeeding.

STAGE 4: TEN TO TWELVE MONTHS

Cow's milk and dairy produce, fish and eggs.

Weaning – *a step-by-step summary*

- Do not start *any* solid foods before four months
- Do not add solid foods to bottles of milk or other drinks
- Give solids from a spoon
- By six months aim for a mixed diet of three small meals a day
- By twelve months your baby should be eating a well-balanced, varied diet that is more or less a chopped-up version of what the rest of the family eats

From bottle to cup

Introduce a cup from six months, with the aim of stopping all feeds from a bottle by the time your baby is one year old. A drinking spout may help this transition, and a beaker with a lid will help prevent spills. Prolonged use of a bottle is inadvisable, as it may delay speech development and food-handling skills. A cup also helps reduce the amount of liquid drunk between meals and so improves babies' appetites, especially if they are faddy eaters.

When to start

Between four and six months is the age when most babies' needs can no longer be met by breastmilk alone. Before the age of four months a baby's digestive tract and excretory system – such as the kidneys – are too immature to cope with solid foods. Neither are a baby's muscles developed enough to enable them to swallow foods safely – or even to move foods from the front to the back of the mouth to swallow. But by four months babies should have enough head and neck control to sit in a chair, and by five months they can take food from a spoon and also pick it up and put it in their mouths, although they cannot feed themselves.

Do not be hurried into weaning by pressure from family and friends who think your baby should be on solids before that time. Start when you and your baby are ready. Signs to look for are:

- Your baby may seem hungry or unsatisfied after a good feed, yet refuse more milk
- Your baby may demand feeds more often
- After sleeping through the night, he or she may start waking in the night, or very early in the morning to be fed

Timing the introduction of solids

The best time to introduce solids is between four and six months, and certainly not before three months. Studies show that babies introduced to solids earlier, from two to three months (eight to twelve weeks), experience more eczema, respiratory illness and persistent coughs from four to six months. Infants given solids too early are also heavier than infants of a similar age who have not received solids.

Premature babies

Seek special advice from your health visitor or family doctor about weaning premature babies, who may need specific help. You may already have encountered problems due to their immature digestive and excretory systems, and they may already have required special nutritional help due to their limited stores of nutrients at birth.

Generally weaning starts when a premature baby weighs around 11lb/5kg and is able to eat from a spoon.

Vegetarian and vegan babies

The process of weaning on to a vegetarian or vegan diet is the same as for other diets. A wide variety of foods from the major food groups should be introduced in the same proportions as for non-vegetarians (see table on page 74). Vegan babies weaned on to a well balanced diet will grow and develop normally, although they are usually smaller and lighter than non-vegans.

Vegetarians who eat dairy foods as part of a mixed diet will receive enough calcium and B vitamins. But for vegans, who avoid dairy foods, it is important to choose soya milk, soya 'cheese' and soya 'yogurt' (and other vegetarian alternatives) that are fortified with vitamins, minerals and calcium. Vegan babies may need supplements of vitamin B12 and riboflavin (B2).

Also take care to ensure at least two servings per day of two of the three sources of vegetarian protein:

- Grains, e.g. rice, wheat, barley, oats, rye, millet, buckwheat and foods made from them (bread, pasta, breakfast cereal), taking the usual precautions about avoiding wheat and other gluten-containing grains before six months
- Pulses, e.g. beans, peas, lentils, chickpeas and soya
- Nuts and seeds, taking the usual precautions about no whole nuts for infants under the age of three.

This can be put into practice simply:

BREAKFAST

Cereal-based

LUNCH/DINNER

Vegetables or pulses with dairy food/vegan alternative (cheese/yoghurt sauce)

LUNCH/DINNER
Fruit with dairy food/vegan alternative

Good combinations of vegetable proteins include familiar foods such as beans on toast, dhal and rice, hummus and pitta bread, lentil soup and bread, rice and beans, pasta with beans. Good non-meat sources of iron include beans, eggs, lentils, green leafy vegetables (spinach, broccoli), bread, fortified breakfast cereals, fortified tofu and dried fruit. But iron from vegetarian sources is less readily available to the body. Food and drink rich in vitamin C (orange juice, citrus fruit, green leafy vegetables, tomatoes, peppers and strawberries among others), eaten at the same time as vegetarian sources of iron, will improve absorption. See page 209 for addresses to write to for further advice.

Twins

Weaning twins should be the same as weaning one baby, and it would be if you had two pairs of hands. But however contented your babies are they will still be quite a handful, especially in the early stages when you are juggling breast/bottle and solids for two babies at the same meal. Different mums have different techniques. Some prefer to feed one baby first and then the other, but often the quickest way is to 'juggle' both at once. Obviously you will need two drinking cups/bottles, but you can get away with one spoon and one large bowl, so long as you ensure that they are getting or taking fair shares. It is really a question of trial and error as to what works best for your family. And remember that what works or is acceptable one day may not be the next, as babies' needs change with their rapid development. You will need more than your fair share of patience, especially as twins will not always be hungry at the same time or like the same foods. You may find yourself handling a disgruntled baby more often than other mothers, but on the other hand you can have twice the fun!

For more advice see Useful Addresses, page 209.

Weaning – Healthy Diet – month by month

	4–6 months Introduce after 4 months	6–9 months	9–12 months	1 year
Dairy	Cow's milk to mix solids, or in yogurt, custard, cheese sauce, after 4 months but not as main drink	500–600ml breast-milk or formula. Cow's milk, as left. Hard cheese as finger food	As left	Minimum 350ml milk daily or *2 servings* cheese, yogurt. Whole milk can now be main drink. Low fat milk in cooking
Starchy foods: bread, pasta, rice, potatoes	Rice cereal blended with milk. Mashed potato or other starchy vegetables	*2–3 servings daily* Introduce wholemeal bread and cereals. Finger food such as toast	*3–4 servings daily* Starchy foods can be normal adult texture	*4 servings daily* At least one serving each meal. Avoid high fat starchy foods e.g. crisps, too many chips, pastry, savoury snacks
Vegetables and fruit	Soft cooked and pureed vegetables and fruit	*2 servings daily* Raw soft fruit and vegetables as finger food. Cooked and mashed vegetables and fruit	*3–4 servings daily* Lightly cooked or raw. Chopped as finger food. Unsweetened orange juice with vegetarian meals	*4 servings daily* Lightly cooked or raw. Unsweetened fruit
Meat and alternatives	Soft cooked and pureed meat and/or pulses	*1 serving daily* Soft cooked and pureed meat and/or pulses	*Minimum 1 serving animal food or 2 from vegetable source* See page 72 re mixing vegetarian protein	*Minimum 1 serving animal food or 2 from vegetable source* Use low fat meat and oily fish (sardine, mackerel)

Weaning and the Weaning Diet, Report of the Committee on Medical Aspects of Food Policy, 1994

Tips for successful weaning

Remember that feeding from a spoon and different tastes are both new to your baby. Take things slowly and do not worry if he or she cries between spoonsful – up to now food has been milk and has come in a continuous uninterrupted stream, but now there are frustrating pauses.

Even if you are anxious for your baby to 'progress' quickly, do not rush and never force feed a baby. Try to avoid spending a lot of time persuading your baby to take food. Talk to your baby during meals – later on you can read stories at mealtimes, if you are not able to eat with your baby and let him or her see you enjoy food, too. Do not make mealtimes too drawn out in your attempts to get your baby to eat more. Babies usually know when they have had enough. They also learn that pudding may come more quickly if they refuse their first course, so it is a good idea only to offer a pudding if the savoury food (or most of it, including the vegetable part when they get older!) is eaten.

How to feed your baby

Sit the baby on your lap for feeds until he or she can sit up comfortably (from six to eight months), when you can transfer to a baby seat or portable first high chair. Start the feed with milk, then offer solids in the middle of the feed when the baby is not quite so hungry. Offer more milk at the end of the meal. After a week or so your baby will get the idea and eat the solids first, then take breast-milk or formula as needed.

Four to six months:
your ABC guide to weaning

A Continue with breastmilk as main food. If using formula still give 600ml a day.

B Offer a small amount of one type of puree at one meal. Offer it after the milk feed or in the middle, depending on what suits your baby best. Your baby may take to solid food quickly or not. Some babies like virtually everything offered to them, while others are more choosy.

C Cow's milk may be used in weaning after four months for cooking foods such as custard and cheese sauce, but not as a drink. From six months yogurt and fromage frais can be given – although if dairy foods are thought to be linked to eczema, for example, wait until ten to twelve months. From one year cow's milk can become a main drink. Up to two years whole or full-fat milk (silver top) is needed for extra calories and the vitamins A and D from the fat in the milk. From the age of two to five semi-skimmed can be given, and after five years skimmed, if your child is eating and growing well.

Please read before you start your baby on the menus that follow

The menus that follow provide plenty of suggestions for the first month of weaning. You do not have to stick to them exactly – you may, for instance, use only half the suggestions, repeating them more often. Go at your baby's pace and follow his or her appetite, which may vary from day to day. And if a food is refused, leave it for a week or more before offering it again. During the second stage of weaning you can use up the batch-cooked and frozen foods you made previously before moving on to more new foods when baby is six months or more.

THE ABC OF HEALTHY EATING FOR BABIES AND TODDLERS

SHOPPING TIP: YOGURT

Full fat fruit yogurts for babies and toddlers are available, but choose with care – they may contain a lot of added sugar and thickeners, and not a lot, or any, fruit. If you cannot find a suitable one, buy a full fat natural (organic) yogurt and stir in home-made fruit puree. This way you avoid unwanted sugar and additives, your baby has the benefit of organic produce and you can control how much fruit you add. The baby can also enjoy more variety because he or she does not have to eat the same flavour yogurt for several meals.

SHOPPING TIP: VEGETABLES

Apricots, broccoli and carrots are excellent fruit and vegetables for your baby to learn to enjoy. They are rich in beta-carotene, a vitamin that protects against cancer and boost the immune system in other ways to help fight infections such as colds and flu.

Drinks for babies

From four months, when solid foods are introduced, babies may need additional drinks to breastfeeds or formula, especially in hot weather. The best drink for babies is cooled boiled water.

Offer drinks other than breastmilk or formula from a spoon for smaller babies, or from a cup or trainer beaker with a spout as soon as your baby can hold one, from six months. Do not offer drinks from a bottle. Keep drinking times short, and never leave baby alone with any drink because of the danger of choking.

One in four parents gives babies unsuitable main drinks such as tea (which reduces the absorption of iron from food, especially if taken with food, and may be constipating), cow's milk or adult fruit drinks such as orange squash. Fruit squash and drinks are unsuitable for babies because they may contain sugar and/or artificial sweeteners and other additives. Artificial sweeteners are not permitted in foods made specifically for babies and young children (that is, those under three years old). Adult drinks may

Day-by-day sample menus: four to six months

	Early morning	Breakfast	Lunch	Dinner	Bedtime
Day 1	Breastmilk	Breastmilk	1 teaspoon apple puree	Breastmilk	Breastmilk
Day 2	Breastmilk	Breastmilk	1 teaspoon apple puree	Breastmilk	Breastmilk
Day 3	Breastmilk	Breastmilk	1–2 teaspoons carrot puree	Breastmilk	Breastmilk
Day 4	Breastmilk	Breastmilk	1–2 teaspoons carrot puree	Breastmilk	Breastmilk
Day 5	Breastmilk	Breastmilk	1–2 teaspoons baby rice	Breastmilk	Breastmilk
Day 6	Breastmilk	Breastmilk	1–2 teaspoons baby rice	Breastmilk	Breastmilk
Day 7	Breastmilk	Breastmilk	1–2 teaspoons ripe banana puree	Breastmilk	Breastmilk
Day 8	Breastmilk	1–2 teaspoons baby rice	1–2 teaspoons potato puree	Breastmilk	Breastmilk
Day 9	Breastmilk	1–2 teaspoons baby rice	1–2 teaspoons ripe banana puree	Breastmilk	Breastmilk
Day 10	Breastmilk	2–3 teaspoons baby rice	2–3 teaspoons pear puree	Breastmilk	Breastmilk
Day 11	Breastmilk	2–3 teaspoons pear puree	2–3 teaspoons carrot puree	Breastmilk	Breastmilk
Day 12	Breastmilk	2–3 teaspoons baby rice	2–3 teaspoons carrot puree	Breastmilk	Breastmilk
Day 13	Breastmilk	2–3 teaspoons baby rice	2–3 teaspoons pumpkin (squash) puree	Breastmilk	Breastmilk
Day 14	Breastmilk	2–3 teaspoons baby rice	2–3 teaspoons carrot puree	Breastmilk	Breastmilk
Day 15	Breastmilk	3–4 teaspoons rice mixed with apple puree	3–4 teaspoons courgette puree	Breastmilk	Breastmilk
Day 16	Breastmilk	3–4 teaspoons rice mixed with pear puree	3–4 teaspoons apple and parsnip puree	Breastmilk	Breastmilk
Day 17	Breastmilk	3–4 teaspoons melon puree	3–4 teaspoons carrot and potato puree	Breastmilk	Breastmilk
Day 18	Breastmilk	3–4 teaspoons melon puree	3–4 teaspoons potato and broccoli puree	Breastmilk	Breastmilk
Day 19	Breastmilk	3–4 teaspoons papaya puree	3–4 teaspoons rice and courgette puree	Breastmilk	Breastmilk
Day 20	Breastmilk	3–4 teaspoons avocado puree	3–4 teaspoons broccoli puree	Breastmilk	Breastmilk
Day 21	Breastmilk	3–4 teaspoons rice with fruit	3–4 teaspoons avocado puree	Breastmilk	Breastmilk
Day 22	Breastmilk	3–4 teaspoons sweet corn puree	3–4 teaspoons potato and spinach puree	Breastmilk	Breastmilk
Day 23	Breastmilk	3–4 teaspoons sweet corn puree	3–4 teaspoons ripe banana and yogurt puree	Breastmilk	Breastmilk
Day 24	Breastmilk	3–4 teaspoons ripe banana puree	3–4 teaspoons yogurt and kiwi puree	Breastmilk	Breastmilk
Day 25	Breastmilk	3–4 teaspoons rice with fruit puree	3–4 teaspoons courgette and carrot puree	Breastmilk	Breastmilk
Day 26	Breastmilk	3–4 teaspoons rice with pear puree	3–4 teaspoons potato and carrot puree	Breastmilk	Breastmilk
Day 27	Breastmilk	3–4 teaspoons rice with papaya puree	3–4 teaspoons parsnip and apple puree	Breastmilk	Breastmilk
Day 28	Breastmilk	3–4 teaspoons rice with prune puree	3–4 teaspoons papaya puree	Breastmilk	Breastmilk

also have a higher sugar content and higher acidity than drinks produced for babies, making them more dangerous for teeth (see page 86).

Some toddlers drink too much saccharin (see page 179) and they could drink too much of another widely used sweetener, aspartame. The presence of aspartame is highlighted on drinks labels because people with a rare condition called phenylketonuria (PKU) cannot break down phenylalanine, found in aspartame and an amino acid in foods containing protein. These people need to follow a low phenylalanine diet. You will know if your baby has PKU because it is tested for in the UK by a heel prick at birth.

Baby fruit juices are better than squash, tea or milk, but are not necessary – even though the manufacturers encourage the idea that babies do not like plain water. As with foods, taste is a learned experience and babies offered exclusively water as an additional drink to breastmilk or formula will drink it when they are thirsty (see also the recommendations on baby food page 61).

Alternatively you could use unsweetened fruit juice, but dilute it well. To start with, from six months, dilute it in the proportions one part juice to ten parts cooled boiled water, increasing gradually to half and half when your child is two. Continue to dilute fruit juice for all pre-school children. Alternatively, consider vegetable juices (without added salt) instead of, or in addition to, fruit juice. Vegetable juices do not usually contain added sugar, some contain more vitamins and minerals than fruit juice, and there are many flavours and colours to appeal to your baby.

Five months: your ABC guide to weaning

A Still offer breastmilk or 500ml formula a day. Breastmilk, formula or cow's milk may be used to mix solids, for instance to moisten baked potato or to thin purees.
B Purees might be slightly thicker. Offer solids at two or three meals a day and increase the variety. Combine two flavours.

C Introduce soft cooked meat such as chicken, lamb or liver and pulses (lentils, split peas). See the recipe section (page 109) for preparation of meat and pulses. Do not introduce wheat and other cereals yet. Continue to introduce more varieties of fruit and vegetables. Include vegetables with all main meals. Dilute the flavours of stronger-tasting vegetables such as cabbage, cauliflower and sprouts by mixing them with sweeter purees such as apple, sweet potato or parsnip, or blander flavours such as potato and rice. Nutritious vegetables such as watercress and spinach can be pureed in with other vegetables.

Six to nine months: your ABC guide to weaning

A Still offer breastmilk or 500ml formula or follow-on formula a day. Breastmilk, formula or cow's milk may be used to mix solids, for instance to moisten baked potato or to thin purees.

B By now your baby should be enjoying a varied and mixed diet. To encourage chewing, food can be coarser in texture and lumpier. And as your baby becomes interested in self-feeding, offer finger foods such as toast or sticks of raw or lightly cooked vegetables on which he or she can chew. Base a mixed diet on the following daily servings: two or three of starchy food, two of fruit and vegetables, and one of meat or an alternative.

C You may now introduce wholemeal bread and other wholegrain cereals such as Weetabix. Get your baby into the habit of eating breakfast cereal, which is an important source of vitamins and minerals (especially the fortified cereals, and there is calcium in milk). Also introduce soft-cooked and pureed or minced fish. If giving diluted fruit juice, restrict it to mealtimes. Continue to avoid nuts, sugar, salt and fatty foods.

SHOPPING TIP: MINCE

While the meat on sale in butcher's and supermarkets should be what it says it is – for example minced steak, beef, lamb or pork – it may be mixed with other meat. Minced lamb has been found to contain minced beef. If possible mince your own, which also allows you to choose leaner cuts.

SHOPPING TIP: PUDDINGS AND SWEETS

Despite baby food manufacturers producing plenty of chocolate puddings there is no need to introduce your baby to chocolate or other sugary or fat-rich puddings yet! Wait until you are forced to do so when, as a toddler, your child is mixing with other children. Even then make chocolate and other confectionery strictly for treats only – and rare treats, at that! However, it has to be said that if, later on, you do allow your toddler sweets (best limited to one or two days a week immediately after meals; see also page 88), then chocolate has a nutritional advantage over some other confectionery because it contains reasonable amounts of iron. However, a lot of British chocolate is made from vegetable fat rather than milk and is not a useful source of calcium.

Time in the kitchen

Do not spend too long preparing elaborate meals for your baby or toddler because you will be frustrated and annoyed if they are not eaten.

Please read before you start your baby on the menus opposite

The menu opposite consists of suggestions only. You do not have to stick to them and you do not have to cook all the meals listed. It may be that your baby is happy and progressing well on one cooked meal a day, preferring sandwiches at the other – in which case simply substitute your preferred choice. You may also want to substitute some commercially prepared baby foods. If so, try to match the main food groups in the meal, for instance replacing meat and vegetables with appropriate foods.

All menus provide recommended daily portions of protein, fruit/ vegetables, carbohydrates and dairy food.

Each menu is repeated, so that if you cook and freeze in week 1 you will have ready-made meals for the next week (and extra portions for later use in many instances).

Pudding, if needed, can be taken with either lunch or dinner. Offer fruit or yogurt for pudding at the other meal.

* = recipe in Chapter 4.

Vitamin Supplements

If breastmilk is still your baby's main drink after six months of age you will need to give him or her supplements of vitamins A and D. These are available from your health visitor at your baby clinic. Formula and follow-on formula is fortified with sufficient vitamins (and minerals).

Can a baby be too fat?

Chubby babies used to be equated with bonny babies, but now that obesity is such a common problem some parents are concerned, even as early as the weaning stage, that their babies are too fat and may grow up into overweight adults.

Day-by-day sample menus: six to nine months

	Early morning	Breakfast	Lunch	Pudding	Dinner	Bedtime
Days 1 and 15	Breastmilk or diluted fruit juice, if needed	Weetabix	*Pasta with tuna and vegetable sauce	Fruit puree (home-made or bought)	*Mashed potato with carrot and cheese	Breastmilk, if needed
Days 2 and 16	As day 1	Ready-brek	*Lamb casserole	Custard with prune puree	*Vegetable risotto	Breastmilk, if needed
Days 3 and 17	As day 1	Porridge	*Macaroni cheese	Orange segments (no pips)	*Chicken with vegetables and rice	Breastmilk, if needed
Days 4 and 18	As day 1	Baby rice and fruit puree	*Lentils Paysanne	*Apricot semolina	*Meatballs and tomato sauce	Breastmilk, if needed
Days 5 and 19	As day 1	Weetabix	*Courgette gratin	Fruit yogurt	*Salmon dinner	Breastmilk, if needed
Days 6 and 20	As day 1	Banana with fromage frais, toast fingers	*Spinach dhal and rice	*Real fruit jelly (or fruit)	*Liver casserole	Breastmilk, if needed
Days 7 and 21	As day 1	Porridge	*Fresh tomato pasta	Fromage frais with fruit	*Tuna risotto	Breastmilk, if needed
Days 8 and 22	As day 1	Weetabix	*Salmon pâté	*Fruit compôte	*Minestrone	Breastmilk, if needed
Days 9 and 23	As day 1	Ready-brek	*Chicken and sweetcorn	Banana and custard	*Lentil and bean cobbler	Breastmilk, if needed
Days 10 and 24	As day 1	Baby rice and fruit	*Spinach and lentil 'pie'	*Fruit fool	*Fish with parsley sauce	Breastmilk, if needed
Days 11 and 25	As day 1	Porridge	*Baked potato	Satsuma segments	*Meatloaf and potatoes	Breastmilk, if needed
Days 12 and 26	As day 1	Weetabix	*Frozen vegetable gratin	Soft berry fruits with vanilla yogurt	*Minced pork with apple sauce	Breastmilk, if needed
Days 13 and 27	As day 1	Ready-brek	Poached cod with potato and broccoli	Egg custard	*Pasta with ricotta	Breastmilk, if needed
Days 14 and 28	As day 1	Baby rice and fruit puree	*Shepherd's pie	*Semolina fruit puree	*Cauliflower cheese	Breastmilk, if needed

All babies should be chubby, and at six months, 25 per cent of their body is fat. This is laid down as an important energy store during weaning to compensate for reduced food intake during illness and periods when babies go off their food, for whatever reason.

So, even if your baby has a hearty appetite and eats everything offered, it is unlikely that there will be a weight problem because (unlike adults) babies stop eating when they are full. However, if you are giving your baby a lot of fatty and sugary foods, you could be encouraging faster weight gain than is desirable. If this is the case, adjust your baby's diet to that outlined in the appropriate-age weaning menu.

But be aware of the difference between sweet and fat-rich foods. A sweet tooth in infancy does not on its own lead to obesity. Obese people are popularly thought to over-eat sweet foods, but this is not necessarily the case; they can have the same preference for sweetness, or greater or less preference. It is more likely that they have a greater preference for higher fat foods.

Do not restrict your baby's food intake unless you are advised to do so by your doctor. Restricting food intake, or putting your baby on an inappropriate low fat, high fibre diet, will have the effect of reducing the infant's intake of vital vitamins and minerals and may seriously slow down his or her rate of growth and development.

Even if your baby were overweight, studies indicate that overweight infants are not overweight as older children or as adults. In fact, 80 per cent or more of obese infants are obese by the age of six. Other studies show that 74 per cent of obese pre-school children are not obese as adults. If you have further concerns, discuss them with your family doctor or health visitor.

Looking after children's teeth

A baby's teeth are vital for chewing and speaking; they keep the spaces needed for the second teeth; and some of them will have to last your child until the age of eleven. If the milk (first) teeth are well looked after it is more likely that the second teeth (which should last

a lifetime, if properly looked after) will grow into their correct position. Looking after teeth will also prevent toothache and a lot of dental work which may be uncomfortable or even painful for your child. And looking after teeth results in a healthy mouth – and happy smiles!

TEETHING PAINS

The pressure of teeth growing through the gums from around six months can cause some babies discomfort and interfere with their eating pattern. There is now scientific evidence that fever does occur in some babies during teething – despite doctors maintaining in the past that there was no evidence to support mothers' reports of temperature, rash, diarrhoea and accompanying retching. A little dental gel containing antiseptic and analgesic (pain reliever) can be gently applied with a fingertip. Between six months and two and a half years all twenty milk teeth will appear. The first are usually the bottom two front teeth, followed by the top two.

Some people's, and therefore babies', teeth are more resistant to dental caries (decay) than others. However, babies and toddlers are at greatest risk because the enamel on their freshly erupted teeth is immature and especially vulnerable. The way to protect them is through a nutritious low sugar diet and regular brushing with fluoride toothpaste.

THE TROUBLE WITH SUGAR

Dental caries, popularly called decay, are caused by acid attacking the enamel of the tooth surface. The acid is produced by bacteria in dental plaque, which is formed from the sugars that we eat. The more often sugar, and sugary food and drink, are consumed, the greater the damage.

About three-quarters of the sugar in the UK diet is added during manufacture and cooking or before we eat food (for instance, spooned on to breakfast cereal). These so-called 'extrinsic' sugars have been extracted from sugar cane or sugar beet to make the sugar used in biscuits, cakes, confectionery, soft drinks, syrups and so on. Stickiness makes matters worse, so biscuits, sweets and other kinds of sugary foods that stick to a baby's teeth are worst. Extrinsic sugars are the main cause of tooth decay, so the types of food that contain them are the ones to limit to avoid tooth decay.

The remaining sugars, known as 'intrinsic' sugars, are naturally present in foods such as milk, fruit and vegetables. While the sugar in fresh fruit, dried fruit and fruit juices is capable of causing dental decay, it is only a very minor cause. These foods should therefore not be limited in your baby's diet.

THE THREAT TO TEETH FROM FRUIT JUICE AND SOFT DRINKS

Soft drinks such as fizzy and fruit drinks (even undiluted fruit juice) taken regularly between meals are dangerous for teeth in another way. They can cause acid erosion, which means that enamel and dentine are attached and dissolved. Enamel is the outer coating of the tooth. It covers a layer of dentine which is another hard substance protecting the inner layer of pulp which contains blood vessels and nerves. Acid erosion is far more difficult to treat than caries. The latest survey of children's teeth shows some decrease in levels of dental decay (probably due to greater use of fluoride toothpaste) but increasing dental erosion.

Most soft drinks have what is called a low pH (meaning they are acidic) and a high titratable acidity (explained below). Fruit-based and fizzy drinks, whether artificially or sugar sweetened, have a pH of between 3 and 4. This is lower than the 'critical' pH of 5.5, below which the tooth enamel can dissolve.

Titratable acidity is measured as the amount of alkali (sodium hydroxide) needed to neutralise the drink. Drinks with a high titratable acidity have more acid present than is indicated by the pH. Many parents are surprised to learn that pure unsweetened fruit juices and some herbal drinks made specifically for babies fall into this category. These drinks can cause dental erosion in the same way as colas and cordial or squash.

In babies and toddlers both types of tooth damage can be caused by giving 'nursing' or 'comforter' bottles. Studies show that children with the highest consumption of fizzy drinks and fruit juice, especially at bedtime, have the most severe tooth erosion.

THE TROUBLE WITH ARTIFICIAL SWEETENERS

Although artificial sweeteners such as saccharin, aspartame, acesulfame and thaumatin are not allowed in foods specifically for babies and young children, they are widely used in foods commonly given to them, for example soft drinks, yogurt, ketchup and even some toothpastes. These artificial sweeteners, present in low sugar or no-added-sugar drinks (and even mixed with sugar in regular food and drink), will not harm teeth. Other sweeteners such as sorbitol, mannitol, xylitol, hydrogenated glucose syrup and isomalt probably do not cause caries either, but sorbitol, mannitol and xylitol can act as laxatives, so do not give too much sugar-free confectionery to pre-school children. Sweets of this sort are not really suitable for children under three, and there is no real reason why they should have them even then.

But though artificial sweeteners may not harm teeth, their presence does not mean that the food and drink which contains them is safe for teeth. Soft drinks in particular (see above) can cause dental erosion.

PREVENTING TOOTH DECAY

Within seconds of sugar entering the mouth, acid is produced by the bacteria in dental plaque and the minerals calcium and phosphate start to be lost from the surface of the teeth. It takes about an hour for the saliva to neutralise the effect of the acid and to begin to replace those lost minerals. Some people – and babies – produce more protective saliva than others. If sugary food such as confectionery, biscuits and other snacks is continuously being put into the mouth the acid will never be neutralised and the minerals

will not be replaced, resulting in decayed teeth that need filling by the dentist.

Eating other foods at the same time as sugar or sugary foods dilutes the acid generated and reduces the harmful effect of the sugar. This is why it is recommended to keep sugary foods to mealtimes. Cheese eaten immediately after sugar makes the mouth less acidic. When cheese sticks to teeth it also provides calcium and phosphorus which can counter the loss of these minerals caused by sugary foods.

Other sugars, such as glucose and glucose syrup, are also dangerous to teeth. So always read the labels on baby drinks, even so-called baby health drinks, and avoid those with sugary ingredients.

STEP-BY-STEP TO HEALTHY TEETH

1. Register your baby with a dentist before the teeth erupt and start taking your baby to the dentist as soon as the dentist agrees. Take your baby and toddler with you when you go for check ups. Make early and regular visits to the dentist a normal event so that your child gets used to regular dental inspections. Children are not born with a fear of going to the dentist – they learn it from adults.
2. Do not give babies dummies dipped in sugary substances. Do not give older babies and toddlers containers of sugar-sweetened fruit drinks or fruit juices for example in the pushchair or when watching TV, to hold during the day, or to take to bed. If a baby has free access to sugary drinks the immature enamel of his or her teeth will be continuously bathed in sugar. Late-night sweets and bedtime biscuits and sweet drinks are particularly bad as the flow of saliva reduces while babies are asleep, leaving bacteria in harmful contact with the teeth all night.
3. Stick to water or milk or very diluted fruit juice between meals.
4. Give toddlers drinking straws or beakers with built-in straws so as to reduce contact between drinks and teeth.
5. Discourage toddlers from swishing sugary or acidic drinks (if they have to have them) around their mouths.

6. Avoid soft drinks, even the low or no added sugar varieties which may still contain sugar in various guises (see page 61) and undesirable artificial sweeteners (below).

7. Do not use sweets or sugary foods such as biscuits as rewards or to prevent tantrums.

8. If you do give your child sugary foods such as biscuits, ice cream, jam and occasional sweets, give them at mealtimes and not between meals.

9. Brush your baby's teeth twice a day with fluoride toothpaste (see below for the right way to brush). Brushing last thing at night is very important. Most children are incapable of the motivation and manual dexterity needed to remove plaque with a toothbrush until they are at least six or seven years of age, so until then parents need to brush their children's teeth for them.

Interestingly, brushing in itself has not been shown to protect teeth effectively as much as using fluoride toothpaste. While brushing is important, its main purpose is to deliver fluoride to the tooth surface.

10. Wait an hour before brushing your baby's teeth after giving him or her acidic food or drink (for example oranges, grapefruit, lemons, citrus juice, fruit squash, fizzy drinks, pickles, yogurt or fruit-based herbal tea). That hour gives the saliva a chance to combat most of the acid, and prevents the acid being brushed all over your child's teeth.

11. Do use a cup as soon as your baby is able to hold one. A drink from a cup is more likely to be drunk all at once, rather than sipped as from a bottle or from a feeder cup with a spout.

12. If you have to allow sweets, for instance because of pressure from older siblings, give them on only one or two days a week. Explain the reason and say that the toddler is being treated in the same way as other children in the family.

13. Ask relatives and friends to find treats other than sweets and biscuits or chocolate confectionery for your children. Comics, stickers, badges, stationery, novelty jewellery, hair slides, hair bands and fun socks will all fit the bill. These items may be more expensive, but they last longer and can be given less frequently than sweets.

Children and tooth decay

More likely:
- Those who take a drink to bed every night, especially if it is a bottle or contains sugar (e.g. squash or juice) rather than milk or water
- Children who eat confectionery daily
- Children who brush unsupervised or who have not had their teeth brushed by an adult

Less likely:
- Children who start having their teeth brushed before the age of one
- Children who brush more than once a day have the least decay

WHICH TOOTHBRUSH?

Start brushing your baby's teeth twice a day, morning and bedtime, as soon as they appear. Use a small baby toothbrush. Children's toothbrushes are labelled with the age range they are designed for, or called milk teeth toothbrushes. For babies use only a smear of children's toothpaste which tastes milder than adults' and contains less fluoride.

BRUSHING THE RIGHT WAY

When brushing babies' and toddlers' teeth use only a pea-size blob of fluoride toothpaste to prevent them ingesting too much fluoride. Teach them to spit out excess paste and rinse after brushing. Stand behind the child and tilt his or her head upwards so all the tooth surfaces can be brushed using a gentle scrub motion, as follows. Place the brush at the base of the tooth and use very short horizontal movements to dislodge plaque from the 'stagnation' areas at the gum margins and between the teeth. Use small movements and gentle pressure, and take your time to clean all the teeth surfaces.

FLUORIDE TABLETS: FOR AND AGAINST

Few children need fluoride supplements. For most, fluoride tooth-paste and a good diet are sufficient to protect their teeth. However, in exceptional circumstances tablets or drops may be advised from the age of six months. This is to ensure that the correct amount of fluoride enters the child's developing teeth and combines with other minerals to strengthen the tooth enamel against decay.

Too much fluoride, however, can damage teeth, giving them a mottled, discoloured appearance. Seek your dentist's advice before giving fluoride tablets, and remember that to be effective they have to be given daily until at least adolescence.

Tooth-friendly snacks

Fresh fruit, fresh vegetables, cheese (small quantities), wholemeal bread, scones or yeasted (low-sugar) buns, whole grain breakfast cereal, milk or no-added-sugar milk shakes.

Nine to twelve months: your ABC guide to weaning

A Continue as before, but increase the amount of food given to suit your baby's appetite. Although breastmilk or 500ml formula or follow-on formula per day is still recommended up to one year, the amount will be reducing as the infant's appetite for other foods grows. Breastmilk, formula or cow's milk may be used to mix solids, for instance to moisten a baked potato or to thin purees.

B Increase the number of portions given as your baby will be hungrier, even though still taking breastmilk or formula. Aim for three to four servings daily of both starchy foods and fruit and vegetables, at least one daily serving of meat or fish or a minimum of two servings from vegetarian sources of protein.

Please read before you start your baby on the menus opposite

The menus opposite consist of suggestions only. You do not have to stick to them and you do not have to cook all the meals listed below. It may be that your baby is happy and progressing well on one cooked meal a day, preferring sandwiches at the other. In this case simply substitute your preferred choice. You may also want to substitute some commercially prepared baby foods. If so, try to match the main food groups in the meal, for instance replacing meat and vegetables with appropriate foods.

All menus provide recommended daily portions of protein, fruit/vegetables, carbohydrates and dairy food.

Each menu is repeated, so that if you cook and freeze in week 1 you will have ready-made meals for the next week (and extra portions for later use in many instances).

If you do not wish to cook, buy the equivalent commercial baby food.

Pudding, if needed, can be taken with either lunch or dinner. Offer fruit or yogurt for pudding at the other meal.

* = recipe in Chapter 4.

Day-by-day sample menus: nine to twelve months

	Early morning	Breakfast	Lunch	Pudding	Dinner	Bedtime
Days 1 and 15	Breastmilk or diluted fruit juice, if needed	Weetabix	*Lasagne with meat and vegetable sauces	Satsuma or orange (no pips)	*Spanish omelette and bread	Breastmilk, if needed
Days 2 and 16	As day 1	Boiled egg with soldiers	*Mushroom risotto	Custard with prune puree	*Broccoli and tuna pasta	Breastmilk, if needed
Days 3 and 17	As day 1	Muffin, toasted or untoasted, and fruit	*Meatloaf II, potato and vegetables	*Rice pudding with dried apricots	*Fish cake with vegetables	Breastmilk, if needed
Days 4 and 18	As day 1	Melon and cereal	*Ham and pea rosti	Fruit salad and frozen yogurt	*Cheese scone	Breastmilk, if needed
Days 5 and 19	As day 1	Weetabix	*Peanut butter sandwiches (page 162)	Yogurt, pear and crumbled crunchy bar	*Lamb shish kebab, vegetables and rice	Breastmilk, if needed
Days 6 and 20	As day 1	Muesli soaked in apple juice overnight	Soup with fingers of cheese on toast	*Raisin bread and butter pudding	*Cod risotto	Breastmilk, if needed
Days 7 and 21	As day 1	Porridge with grated fresh fruit or berries	*Lamb and bean hotpot with potatoes	Apricot semolina	*Avocado risotto	Breastmilk, if needed
Days 8 and 22	As day 1	Weetabix	*Tabbouleh	Milk lolly and fruit	*Pommes Anna with liver	Breastmilk, if needed
Days 9 and 23	As day 1	Boiled egg with soldiers	*Potato and watercress soup with bread	Fromage frais and fruit	*Ratatouille and pasta	Breastmilk, if needed
Days 10 and 24	As day 1	Toasted muffin and fruit	Baked potato with filling of choice	Fruit fool or yogurt	*Lean burger with vegetables	Breastmilk, if needed
Days 11 and 25	As day 1	Porridge with fruit puree	*Cod in parsley sauce and potatoes	Satsuma or orange	*Sweetcorn and cheese fritter	Breastmilk, if needed
Days 12 and 26	As day 1	Weetabix	Welsh rarebit and vegetable sticks	Fresh fruit and vanilla yogurt	*Fishballs in tomato and vegetable sauce	Breastmilk, if needed
Days 13 and 27	As day 1	Ready-brek	*Cheese polenta with tomato sauce	Banana rice	*Baked potato 'pizza'	Breastmilk, if needed
Days 14 and 28	As day 1	Porridge	*Pasta with poached salmon	*Apple sponge and custard	*Potato parmigiana	Breastmilk, if needed

C   There is still no need to give chocolate and sweets, and no need for packet desserts, ice creams, cartons of fatty and sugary chilled desserts such as chocolate mousse, creme caramel, trifle and so on – except for occasional treats. See Nutritious Bakes in Chapter 4 for alternatives.

Sandwiches from nine months

Use soft wholemeal bread and cut off the crusts. Make the fillings moist and cut into small squares or fingers. Suggestions for fillings are on page 161.

From one to two years old: your ABC guide to feeding younger toddlers

A   Milk is still an important source of calories and calcium for most toddlers, but less is needed. Continue with breastfeeding, if appropriate, but do not give more than 350ml formula or follow-on formula because more will reduce your child's appetite for food. Full fat milk can now be the main drink. Give milk from a cup, and discourage feeding from a bottle after one year. If your child does not like milk try two daily servings of dairy produce such as yogurt, cheese, cheese sauce, custard or fromage frais. Or find a suitable vegetarian alternative such as soya milk, oat milk or rice milk.
B   Further increase servings to a minimum of four daily of starchy foods, the same of fruit and vegetables, plus one serving of animal protein or two of vegetarian protein.
C   Snacks may now be needed between meals, but not at the expense of three meals a day. Offer fruit (fresh or dried) or bread (no need to spread anything on it) or a low fat, low sugar bun such as a wholemeal hot cross bun, or vegetables. Limit juice to mealtimes. Continue to avoid chocolate and sweets, and so on.

Expand the choice to include Shredded Wheat (or mini-wheats), which does not contain added fat and sugar but before the age of one is difficult to eat unless it is well soaked or broken up. In addition try Puffed Wheat, muesli (luxury types with lots of dried fruit but be careful of whole nuts in some muesli which is unsuitable for toddlers under three), and some that are still nutritionally valuable but contain a little added sugar: Sustain, puffed rice, Raisin Splitz and cornflakes.

MILK AND MEALS FROM 1 YEAR

If you have not already done so, now is a good time to dispense with bottles. Although milk can become the main drink at 12 months, replacing formula or breastmilk, it is easy to get into bad habits with bottles of milk. For example: leaving a toddler with a bottle at bedtime, or encouraging bottles of milk at bedtime. While milk is a nutritious food it should not be taken in large volume because it will reduce your toddler's appetite for food. Adjusting the quantity of milk is an important part of weaning and establishing good eating habits. If you have not already swapped your baby from bottle to cup, this is the time to do it. The longer you leave weaning from a bottle the harder it will become. It may seem a long way off, but if by two years, or older in some cases, your toddler is still having one or more bottles of milk at bedtime (or during the night) you will find it very hard to potty train your child out of night-time nappies. Toddlers who drink large amounts at night or during the night cannot be expected to be dry without nappies. You will also find that your toddler is more likely to be a picky eater or just not interested in food because the appetite is being satisfied with milk.

If you wish to continue with a bedtime drink of milk (which is certainly preferable to juice after teeth have been cleaned), offer it in a cup only, or to start with, a cup with a spout. Or make water the bedtime drink, with occasional cups of milk to settle a wakeful or hungry toddler in the night.

Please read before you start your baby on the menus that follow

The menus outlined below consist of suggestions only. You do not have to stick to them and you do not have to cook all the meals listed below. It may be that your baby is happy and progressing well on one cooked meal a day, preferring sandwiches at the other. In this case simply substitute your preferred choice. You may also want to substitute some commercially prepared baby foods for toddlers – although by now your baby will really have outgrown baby food and, to satisfy his or her appetite, the necessary quantity of commercially prepared foods will work out very expensive. If you do use them, as before try to match the main food groups in the meal, such as replacing meat and vegetables with appropriate foods.

All the menus provide recommended daily portions of protein, fruit/vegetables, carbohydrates and dairy food, although you can give more fruit each day than is shown here.

Each menu is repeated, so that if you cook and freeze in week 1 you will have ready-made meals for the next week (and extra portions for later use in many instances).

Pudding, if needed, can be taken with either lunch or dinner. Offer fruit or yogurt for pudding at the other meal.

* = recipe in Chapter 4.

Day-by-day sample menus: one to two years

	Early morning	Breakfast	Lunch	Pudding	Dinner	Bedtime
Days 1 and 15	Breastmilk or diluted fruit juice if needed	Breakfast cereal and toast, to suit appetite.	Carrot soup with bread or roll and fruit	Satsuma or orange (no pips)	*Mackerel salad	Breastmilk, if needed
Days 2 and 16	As day 1	Sometimes cereal (with fresh or dried	Rye bread, soft cheese and strawberries	*Raisin bread and butter pudding	Chicken casserole	Breastmilk, if needed
Days 3 and 17	As day 1	fruit) is enough to start with and toast can	Bagel with soft cheese and avocado	Rice pudding with dried apricots	*Salmon quiche with vegetables	Breastmilk, if needed
Days 4 and 18	As day 1	be offered later in the morning or as a mid-morning	Ham and pea soup with bread	Mango hedgehog	Roast lamb and vegetables with new potatoes	Breastmilk, if needed
Days 5 and 19	As day 1	snack. Or offer the selection of	Pitta bread, tabbouleh	Yogurt	*Chicken stir fry	Breastmilk, if needed
Days 6 and 20	As day 1	breakfasts from the 9–12	Chicken sandwich	*Real fruit jelly and custard	*Home-made pizza	Breastmilk, if needed
Days 7 and 21	As day 1	month menu: boiled egg with soldiers,	*Prawn and potato 'curry'	Fruit salad and malt loaf	Scotch egg and vegetables	Breastmilk, if needed
Days 8 and 22	As day 1	muffin, melon, Weetabix, porridge,	*Red pepper soup and sandwich	Date bar and yogurt	Tortellini with vegetable and tomato sauce	Breastmilk, if needed
Days 9 and 23	As day 1	toasted muffin etc.	*Crumbed cod steak	Fromage frais and fruit	*Frittata or omelette	Breastmilk, if needed
Days 10 and 24	As day 1		Baked potato	*Spoonable milkshake	Grilled chicken with vegetables and potatoes	Breastmilk, if needed
Days 11 and 25	As day 1		Ham, cheese and tomato topped muffin	Satsuma or orange segments (no pips)	Noodles with sesame seed and stir fry vegetables	Breastmilk, if needed
Days 12 and 26	As day 1		Apple, grape and soft cheese sandwich	Fresh fruit and vanilla yogurt	*Gnocchi in tomato and vegetable sauce	Breastmilk, if needed
Days 13 and 27	As day 1		*Lamb with squash and lentils	Sorbet and wafer or milk lolly	*Potato apple pancake	Breastmilk, if needed
Days 14 and 28	As day 1		Ham and coleslaw	*Apple crumble and yogurt	*Roast fish and vegetables	Breastmilk, if needed

Two to three years:
your ABC guide to feeding older toddlers

A Milk will be far less important now, contributing fewer calories. If you are confident that your child is obtaining enough calories you can switch to semi-skimmed milk until the age of five, when you can switch to skimmed.

B Continue to serve a minimum of four daily portions of starchy foods, the same of fruit and vegetables, plus one serving of animal protein or two of vegetable protein. Fruit, vegetables and starchy foods become increasingly important during the second year of life, when your child's growth slows down and the need for high calorie foods decreases. This does not, however, mean that small children need a low fat and high fibre diet. They still have small stomachs and large energy, vitamin and mineral needs that demand a nutrient-dense diet.

C Breakfast, and breakfast cereals, form an important part of a young child's diet. Breakfast cereals provide up to 30 per cent of the calories in the diets of children aged between one and a half and four and a half, provide 48 per cent of their iron, and are an important source of other minerals and vitamins, especially calcium, mainly because milk is eaten with them. But high fibre cereals such as All-Bran, Bran Buds, Bran Flakes, Sultana Bran and Fruit 'N' Fibre are still not suitable and should not be given to children under the age of two. See shopping tip page 95.

Letting go

You are now at the stage where complete control over what your child eats may be losing out to influences from nursery school, friends, parties and so on. If you explain simply why you choose certain foods and avoid others, either completely, or have them infrequently, your child may go along with you to a certain extent. And you can make up for deficiencies and deviations at home. For example, if they have biscuits at Nursery School, do not have them at home. If you don't buy them, your child can't have them!

Please read before you start your baby on the menus overleaf

The menus overleaf consist of suggestions only. You do not have to stick to them and you do not have to cook all the meals listed here. It may be that your child is happy and progressing well on one cooked meal a day, preferring sandwiches at the other. In this case simply substitute your preferred choice.

All the menus provide recommended daily portions of protein, fruit/vegetables, carbohydrates and dairy food, but give toddlers extra fruit as required.

Each menu is repeated, so that if you cook and freeze in week 1 you will have ready-made meals for the next week (and extra portions for later use in many instances).

* = recipe in Chapter 4.

Day-by-day sample menus: two to three years and beyond

	Breakfast	Lunch	Pudding	Dinner	Snacks
Days 1 and 15	As before, plus muesli,	Sandwiches with crudités and fruit	Yogurt and granola	*Chicken in peanut butter sauce	Fresh fruit e.g. apple, pear,
Days 2 and 16	muffins, milkshakes, pancakes with fruit puree.	Toasted sandwiches and crudités or fruit slices	Baked apple with dried fruit filling	Meatballs in tomato and vegetable sauce	banana, grapes, orange. Dried fruit e.g. apricots, raisins, peaches,
Days 3 and 17	Occasional treats of	Pizza	Fruit salad and yogurt	Chops, grilled with vegetables	pears, papaya, figs, prunes.
Days 4 and 18	croissant (no spread) and other	Quiche with carrot and nut salad	*Mango hedgehog and orange slices	Chicken breast with vegetables and new potatoes	Vegetable sticks. Fruit cake (no icing).
Days 5 and 19	continental pastries, as	Sardines on toast	Pancake and fruit puree	Grilled salmon with vegetables	Wholemeal scones and buns.
Days 6 and 20	before	Tuna and soft cheese dip with vegetables and bread	Real fruit brûlée	Liver casserole	Rice cakes. Crispbread. Breadsticks. *Treats* Cereal
Days 7 and 21		Baked potato and prawns	Blancmange	Chicken satay sticks, vegetables and rice	bar, gingerbread, carrot cake,
Days 8 and 22		Seafood-filled pancake	Date and orange salad	Baked beans on toast	flapjack, cheesecake.
Days 9 and 23		Mashed sardines and soft cheese on toast	Cheesecake	Oven-baked ribs in sweet and sour sauce with vegetables and rice	Milk, if needed
Days 10 and 24		Baked potato with grated cheese and vegetables	Milkshake with frozen yogurt and fruit	Fish risotto with vegetables	
Days 11 and 25		Sausage and mashed potato	Satsuma or orange segments	Noodles with prawns and vegetables	
Days 12 and 26		Gnocchi in tomato sauce	Fresh fruit and vanilla yogurt	Fishcakes in parsley sauce with potatoes and vegetables	
Days 13 and 27		Toasted raisin bread sandwiches	Fruit compôte and custard	Chicken and vegetable pie with vegetables	
Days 14 and 28		Sandwiches with vegetable sticks and fruit slices	Stewed apple and yogurt	Shepherd's pie with vegetables	

Eating up greens

Even the baby who ate up all his or her vegetables during weaning may become picky about vegetables as a toddler. This is very common, and is associated with learning to make choices and becoming more independent. While they are bound to have some preferences and a few definite dislikes which should be respected – unlike the general childish exclamation, 'Yuck, vegetables!' – it is important to try to include a wide range of vegetables in your child's diet. If he or she refuses all or some you will have to hide vegetables in pasta sauces, pizza toppings, flan fillings, casseroles, soups and so on. Try offering raw vegetables (carrots, pepper, cucumber, tomato, celery) with sandwiches or grated into sandwich fillings.

However, new tastes can be learned, especially if the parents set an example by eating up their vegetables! Continue to serve (small) portions of vegetables at meals. In other words, do not only offer foods which your child is eager and quick to eat. Persist with vegetables.

If your toddler goes through a period of vegetable refusal, try sweeter vegetables such as sweet potatoes, parsnips and carrots, and give the child more fruit, and consider a vitamin and mineral supplement if necessary. At the same time, while not making an issue of any particular food, do not allow a child who refuses to eat any vegetables to have pudding. Without a major confrontation, it is possible to enforce one simple rule: No Vegetables, No Pudding.

And don't just take my word for it . . . 'Cancer fears as children refuse to eat their greens' . . . 'Parents lose battle with the greens' . . . Just two headlines following publication of a Cancer Research Campaign report highlighting the poor eating habits of children and the potential health risks of such a diet. The report warned of the consequences when parents give up trying to get their children to eat vegetables. In some cases children only ate fresh vegetables once a year, at Christmas dinner. Mums interviewed for the report were aware that vegetables contribute to general good health, but they did not know of the connection between eating them and cancer prevention. They said their children's eating habits were worrying, but they were not prepared to set a good example in their eating habits or enforce stricter rules at mealtimes. Many parents never sat down to eat with their children.

The truth is that children will eat vegetables – and learn to enjoy them. So don't just take it from me . . . read this extract from a letter written by Dr Laurence Villard of Oxford which appeared in *The Independent* in response to the above news item. The key points are No Vegetables, No Pudding; and absolute consistency.

> I am a nutritionist with two children aged seven and four. I succeeded in both cases [to get them to eat their greens], and this is how it worked.
>
> They never touched a jar of baby food. From breast-feeding they were weaned on simple, home-made foods – pureed apple, carrot or rice – then the same food as we ate. All meals eaten at home are a family occasion.
>
> Nowadays they eat most vegetables and fruits. Sometimes they go off one or another for a time, and we don't insist. We had a few very short-lived battles in the early days, solved by making them eat the vegetable first before moving on to the rest of the meal.
>
> There was no question of disguising taste – this does not solve the problem. We were absolutely consistent and the battles didn't last. They never starved themselves in retaliation, either.

Let's give the last word on the subject to columnist Bel Mooney in the *Daily Mail*:

> The fact is, parenting is largely about instruction. It requires accepting a 'given' – like the fact that Food A is far better than Food B, and then having the energy, wisdom, common sense and love to insist that therefore there can be no choice . . .
>
> . . . Mealtimes at home and at school do not have to be scenes of stressful anarchy. With the right disciplines imposed, they can be a source of universal good . . .

THE ABC OF HEALTHY EATING FOR BABIES AND TODDLERS

. . . let us return, at home and at school, to a national philosophy which says that the prime right of every parent is to tell a child what to do — and what to eat.

Picky eaters

Many toddlers and young children refuse food, especially when they learn what an explosive effect it can have on their parents! Small children's appetites also vary from day to day, depending on how active they have been and so on. And with small stomachs they are unable to eat large meals. All this makes their eating less predictable than 'conditioned' adult appetites, which are governed more by habit and circumstance than by real tummy-rumbling hunger. If you think your child is eating very little, bear in mind that expected weight gain between the ages of one and four years is only around 2kg/5lbs a year. However, if you are worried that your child is failing to gain weight or is losing weight consult your family doctor or health visitor.

STRATEGIES FOR COPING WITH PICKY EATERS

Parents are naturally distressed if a child is not eating well. This can easily lead to arguments and tension, which make mealtimes unpleasant. In addition, punishing children for not eating, or forcing them to eat, will make everyone unhappy and will not improve the situation. If your child is a consistently fussy eater consider some of the following ploys.

TIME IT RIGHT
Leaving meals until a child is overtired or too hungry will result in him or her refusing to eat, or eating very little.

BE CAREFUL WITH SNACKS BETWEEN MEALS
Always remember that toddlers have small stomachs and unreliable appetites. While snacks between meals can be helpful in achieving a

balanced diet, for example providing opportunities to offer nutritious fruit or wholemeal bread/buns, they can also be detrimental if they consist of fatty or sugary foods. Whether nutritious or not, a mid-morning or mid-afternoon snack can also take the edge off the child's appetite for main meals. If this applies to your situation, try cutting out snacks.

DO NOT LET THEM FILL UP ON DRINK

Some toddlers and young children are not hungry at mealtimes because they fill themselves up with drinks between meals. Children may even prefer drinking to eating because it is quicker, leaving them more time for playing. If this is the case, avoid giving drinks for at least one hour before a meal and do not put a drink on the table until at least halfway through a meal, or even afterwards. This way hunger should be satisfied with food rather than liquid.

DO NOT FORCE THE ISSUE

If after a reasonable time your child has not eaten anything, take the meal away. Try to do it calmly and without anger, no matter how much time and effort you put into shopping and cooking. Do not contrive ways of keeping them at the table until they have eaten. Simply remove the meal without fuss. Do not offer any other food until the next meal. It is important not to give in and offer biscuits, crisps, confectionery or other treats. Stick to this rule, as it will also help establish regular mealtimes.

ESTABLISH REGULAR MEALTIMES

Setting a regular time and place for meals helps to establish a pattern of eating. So do not undo the good work you did during weaning, establishing three meals a day from the chaotic beginnings of demand feeding! However, if mealtimes are long – for example when you have guests or when all the family are present and busy chatting – allow a toddler to leave the table between courses if necessary.

HELP THEM EAT MORE EASILY

Giving children their own set of small cutlery should enthuse them, and also make it easier for them to eat – although fingers will probably be the preferred tool! Either way, cut the food up into small pieces, and help them if they are tired or having difficulty. The right atmosphere will also facilitate eating. If possible eat in family groups, so that a toddler feels that he or she is joining in with a 'grown-up' activity. When this is not possible, make sure there are no distractions such as television during mealtimes, although reading a story to them can sometimes help. Help them concentrate on the meal by using jolly children's plates and cups or beakers and place mats. The characters and pictures on them can often be a topic of conversation that will keep a child's interest in the meal.

LET THEM HELP COOK AND PREPARE FOOD

If children have had a hand in preparing a meal they are more likely to eat it. Having a three-year-old as a sous-chef in the kitchen may slow your progress considerably and cause a mess, but it is valuable learning experience for a child and it is fun. To reduce mess, let toddlers 'work' on a tray so that spills are contained. They may just like to have a jug and cup of water to pour, with an occasional 'taste' of what you are doing.

DO NOT MAKE FOOD FACES ON THE PLATE

I cannot find any evidence to support the tired old advice churned out by most books and sources of advice, which suggest that fussy eaters will suddenly find an appetite if their plate of sausage, peas and mash, or their pizza topping, takes on the guise of a ridiculous face. Most mothers are too busy to waste their time turning pears into mice or bacon and egg into a surrealist landscape. Food is food, and should be respected and enjoyed as such by adults and toddlers. The surroundings, activities and conversation should be the sources of fun.

To avoid confrontational situations eat in a new environment (not in front of the television). Try going for a picnic, or else eat in the garden or your local park.

What to do about an overweight child

Living in a culture of slimming and diets, parents may naturally think that a diet is the solution to their child's weight problem. It is not. Putting a toddler or pre-school child on a slimming diet is the last thing you should do. Even older children and adolescents should not diet – although it is a 'normal' pastime for teenage girls.

The sensible approach is to encourage a healthy diet, which means looking at the types of food your child is eating. Do not cut down on what your child eats, but alter the proportion of foods eaten. If foods from the four main food groups (potatoes, bread, pasta, rice, breakfast cereal and other cereals; vegetables and fruit; low fat dairy food; and fish, lean meat and poultry or vegetarian alternative – (for more detail see the table on page 74) form 99 per cent of the diet, they will squeeze fatty (and fattening) foods out of the diet. Less nutritious and higher calorie foods such as sweets and other confectionery, biscuits, cakes, puddings, sugary drinks, ice cream, crisps and other savoury snacks, meat pies and pastries should be for occasional treats.

Over time, adjusting the diet in this way will maintain your child's health and allow for growth and development without contributing surplus weight. It is particularly important to get children of all ages into the habit of eating breakfast and sticking to three meals a day, with minimal snacks (which should always be nutritious ones). As your child grows, the rate of weight gain will slow down until he or she has grown into the extra weight they put on!

This is a far healthier approach than following the Duchess of York's disastrous example of putting her daughter on a diet. Any 'slimming' diet for a child should be supervised by a dietitian or your family doctor and is rarely resorted to. If you restrict food (other than the unsuitable snacks above) your child may not obtain all the nutrients needed for growth and development.

Allowing your child plenty of time and space for energetic play and exercise will also help to prevent weight problems, and improve bone strength and general health.

Constipation

If toddlers become constipated it is often because of inadequate fibre intake. However, this does not mean that toddlers should be on a high fibre diet or be given raw bran. Such a diet would be too bulky to provide enough calories for growth, and bran can prevent minerals being absorbed. Eating enough vegetables and fruit daily, as outlined in the menus, should prevent constipation. However, all the following situations can lead to constipation:

A lot of travel

Change in environment and timetable (for instance holidays)

Stress

Upset leading to irregular mealtimes

Side-effects of medicines

Poor appetite

Lack of exercise due to illness

In any of these situations, try one of the following gentle remedies:

Swap to wholemeal bread/pasta and to brown rice (if this is not already the norm)

Increase fresh fruit intake

Chop a couple of prunes into breakfast cereal or dessert

Give your toddler a small glass of freshly squeezed orange juice or prune juice

Increase the amount of water drunk

Include more bean/lentil recipes until the problem sorts itself out

If the problem persists take your child to your family doctor.

Diet and IQ

The link between diet, nutrition and IQ caused enormous controversy in the 1980s when a study claimed that the non-verbal IQ of British

schoolchildren could be improved if they took vitamin and mineral supplements. In other words, children with a higher vitamin and mineral intake did better in exams and with written work at school. Replica studies failed to substantiate the initial findings, and researchers are still arguing over the statistical significance of these studies.

In the meantime, parents who are wondering whether their children's academic performance could be improved by vitamin and mineral tablets might do better to look to recent studies carried out in Asia, Africa and South America, where the so-called Green Revolution has had a negative effect on children's IQ. The Green Revolution introduced high-yielding cereal crops and Western agro-chemical techniques so that food intake in some Third World countries has increased – but at a price. There may be more food available, but it lacks the essential vitamins and minerals which were contained in the vegetables, fruit and other local food grown previously using traditional methods of agriculture. In particular more iron, zinc and beta-carotene (vitamin A) deficiencies have occurred, causing debilitating tiredness, anaemia, poor concentration and poor mental and motor skills in pre-school and primary school children, which leaves them incapable of learning. So although fewer people in these countries are actually dying of starvation, the dietary 'improvements' have reduced intellect and immunity.

In the UK the only vitamin supplements recommended for pre-school children are drops containing vitamins A, C and D, handed out by health visitors and GPs as a safeguard if a child's diet is thought to be inadequate. However, 'fringe' research continues into whether children eating what is considered an adequate diet are obtaining enough vitamins and minerals to reach their highest potential non-verbal IQ. The nutrients thought to be of particular significance in this area are vitamins C, B3, B6 and B1, plus the minerals iron and magnesium. If you are considering a dietary supplement for your child it is probably best to discuss the necessity or safety of this venture with your GP or health visitor.

CHAPTER 4

Recipes

Every recipe you need from starting on solids to feeding a pre-school child

Ten Golden Food Safety Rules

1. Store raw meat, poultry and fish at the bottom of the fridge in a deep dish, not a plate. This prevents any drips containing bacteria from contaminating other food, especially food that is not going to be cooked or heated before it is eaten.

2. Keep raw and cooked food apart to prevent cross-contamination (as above).

3. Wash chopping boards, knives and other equipment such as dishcloths after they have been used to prepare raw food. Let equipment drip-dry rather than wiping it with a teatowel that might contain bacteria. Better still, have a dedicated chopping board for raw meat.

4. Wash your hands repeatedly before food preparation, during it and after every interruption, whether you are just answering the telephone, or you have changed the baby or gone to the lavatory.

5. Cook food thoroughly to kill any microbes that may be present in it. And eat cooked foods immediately – as soon as they are cool enough not to burn the baby's mouth – before they reach room

temperature, at which bacteria multiply quickly if food is left standing around.

6. Cool food quickly if it is to be frozen or stored in the fridge for later use. As soon as it is cool, cover it and put it in the fridge or freezer.

7. If food is being kept hot (which is not good practice), keep it at above 63°C.

8. Do not keep or use food beyond its best-before date. It may deteriorate and become harmful even if it tastes all right. And a baby cannot tell you that it tastes peculiar.

9. Keep all food and drinks covered to protect them from flies and other insects which carry germs that could give a baby a nasty tummy upset.

10. Keep pets off work surfaces because their feet often carry undesirable bacteria including salmonella. Always wash your hands – and those of your child – after touching pets and their litter trays, and especially before preparing or eating food.

Recipe servings

Many of the recipes in this chapter are suitable for all the family and most (from the age of six months) are made in family-size quantities, because you do not want to have to cook once for the baby and again for yourself or the rest of the family. As the aim of weaning is to accustom your baby to eating the same food as the rest of the family, it makes sense to eat more or less the same food for everyday meals.

Ingredients

I recommend using organic ingredients wherever possible, especially for staple foods such as milk, cheese, yogurt, eggs, bread, breakfast cereal, pasta, rice, flour, vegetables, fruit and meat. Use vegetable oils and margarine high in polyunsaturates and which contain vitamin E as an antioxidant.

THE ABC OF HEALTHY EATING FOR BABIES AND TODDLERS

None of the recipes up to one year includes added salt or added sugar. If you wish to continue a sugar-free regime after that time this is admirable, although too difficult for most people, and not to their taste, although enjoying food with less, or no, added salt is possible, over time. Once you do it you will be amazed how salty 'normal' food tastes. The pudding and baking recipes for toddlers do contain some added sugar, but the items have been chosen for their nutrient-rich ingredients and their relatively small amount of sugar compared with confectionery and comparable commercial products.

Four to six months

Hygiene reminder: before preparing baby food, especially for babies under six months, please read the notes on hygiene and baby food preparation in Chapter 3 (page 65). Also check the Ten Golden Food Safety Rules at the beginning of this chapter.

Apple puree

Peel, core and slice an eating apple. Put it in a saucepan with 2–3 tablespoons water to prevent sticking or burning. Cover with a lid and cook over a low to moderate heat until the apple slices are soft – about 5 minutes, depending on how thin the slices are. Push the cooked apple through a sieve or mouli, or blend to a puree in a liquidiser. Allow to cool completely before offering to your baby.

COOKING TIP
Prepare 6 apples at a time and freeze the puree in ice cube trays.

Carrot puree

Make as for apple puree (above), but use just enough water to cover the sliced carrots as they cook. Be careful not to let the pan boil dry and burn.

Baby rice

Either make a thin porridge of ground or flaked rice, or make up baby rice adding the quantity of liquid (expressed breastmilk, formula or cooled boiled water) as instructed on the pack. Alternatively, use cornmeal, sago or millet, but not wheat, oats, barley or rye. (See also Shopping Tip on page 68).

Potato puree

Either make as for carrot puree (above), using peeled and chopped potatoes, or sieve/mouli the flesh only of a baked potato. Moisten the potato with expressed breastmilk, formula or cooled boiled water.

Banana puree

Peel and mash a ripe banana with a fork, then mix well with a spoon to soften the texture further. Do this just before feeding your baby as banana discolours and deteriorates quickly. A drop of lemon juice will slow this process.

Banana and yogurt puree

Mash the banana with natural yogurt or fromage frais.

Pear puree

Either make as for apple puree (page 111) if the pears are hard, or mouli/mash ripe and juicy raw pears.

THE ABC OF HEALTHY EATING FOR BABIES AND TODDLERS

Pumpkin (or other varieties of squash) puree

Make as for carrot puree (page 111), but cube the pumpkin flesh. Alternatively, pierce the skin of a whole pumpkin or similar vegetable such as butternut squash, and bake it in a moderate oven. Put the pierced pumpkin in a shallow dish, as a small amount of liquid will ooze from it during baking. Test by inserting the point of a sharp knife or a skewer. When the flesh is soft, remove the pumpkin from the oven and cut in half. When cool enough to handle, scoop out the seeds and discard them. Push the flesh through a sieve or mouli, or blend to a puree in a liquidiser. Allow to cool completely before offering to your baby.

Courgette puree

Steam unpeeled and sliced courgettes, then pass through a sieve/ mouli.

Apple and parsnip puree

Make parsnip puree as for carrot puree (page 111). Stir in equal quantities of apple puree (page 111).

Melon puree

Sieve/mouli the flesh of a ripe melon.

Potato and broccoli puree

Steam florets of broccoli, and when tender sieve/mouli. Mix 1 part broccoli with 2 parts potato puree (page 112).

Papaya puree

Sieve, mouli or mash ripe papaya. Prepare only the quantity to be used just before serving – it will not keep. Optional: add 1 drop fresh lime juice for flavour.

Rice and courgette puree

Mix equal quantities of courgette puree (above) and baby rice made up in the usual way (page 112).

Avocado puree

Sieve, mouli or mash ripe avocado. Prepare only the quantity to be used and do so just before serving – it will not keep. Optional: add 1 drop lemon juice to prevent discolouration.

Sweetcorn puree

Sieve/mouli the drained and rinsed contents of a can of sweetcorn kernels (canned without added sugar or salt).

SHOPPING TIP: CANNED PRODUCE
Purees served as weaning food can be made from additive-free, unsweetened fruit canned in water or juice, or unsalted and unsweetened vegetables canned in water (not brine).

Potato and spinach puree

If using fresh spinach, wash the leaves well and put them into a saucepan with no extra water. Cook over a moderate heat until tender. Sieve or mouli 1 part spinach with 2 parts potato puree (page 112).

For a quicker version use a bag of ready-washed microwave-in-the-bag spinach from a supermarket and follow the instructions on the pack.

Yogurt and kiwi puree

Blend the flesh in a liquidiser with natural yogurt. Prepare just before serving and make only the quantity to be used – it will not keep.

Courgette/carrot and potato puree

Combine equal quantities of all three purees (pages 111–13).

Prune or dried apricot puree

Cook either ready-to-eat or standard fruit (soak the latter first, as instructed on the pack) in enough water to cover them, in a pan with a lid. When very tender, leave to cool in the cooking liquid. Remove stones, if necessary – always check prunes for stones even if the pack says they have already been stoned. Liquidise in a blender, then sieve/mouli for babies four to six months, after which liquidising is sufficient.

Six to nine months

Pasta with tuna and vegetable sauce

½ red pepper, deseeded and chopped
15ml / 1 tablespoon vegetable oil
2 carrots, sliced
115g/4oz French *or* string *or* runner beans, sliced
2 large tomatoes, skinned, and deseeded and chopped
1 courgette, sliced
55g/2oz wholemeal pasta
115g/4oz tuna canned in water

Put the pepper half under a hot grill, skin side uppermost. When the skin is black and charred allow it to cool, then remove the skin and slice the pepper beneath. Heat the oil in a pan and add the vegetables. Cover the pan and sweat over a low to medium heat for 10 minutes, stirring occasionally to prevent sticking. Add about 300ml/½ pint water or no-added-salt vegetable stock. Add the pasta and cook for a further 15 minutes until the pasta is cooked. Transfer to a food processor/liquidiser/mouli. Drain the tuna and add. Blend to the desired consistency, or chop for older babies. Cool quickly and portion for freezing.

Mashed potato with carrot and cheese

Either boil some peeled potatoes and cook in the usual way, or bake jacket potatoes and remove the flesh. Mash the flesh with a little milk, some natural yogurt or soft white cheese to moisten. If you use milk, add a little finely grated cheese while the potato is warm so that it melts into the flesh, then stir in very finely grated carrot.

Lamb casserole

3 medium potatoes *or* sweet potatoes, sliced
175g/6oz neck fillet of lamb, chopped
1 leek, washed, trimmed and sliced
1 courgette, sliced
2 carrots, grated

Put the potatoes in the base of a heavy pan. Lay the lamb, leek and courgette on top. Add the carrots. Cover with water, bring to the boil and then reduce the heat to simmering point. Cook gently, topping up with water if necessary, for 35 minutes. Transfer to a processor/mouli and blend to the desired consistency, or chop for older babies. Cool quickly and portion for freezing.

Vegetable risotto

NB   Although brown rice is nutritionally superior and should be the 'everyday' rice of the household, arborio (or risotto) rice makes a much better risotto.

15ml/1 tablespoon olive
oil *or* other vegetable oil
55g/2oz arborio rice
4 mushrooms, sliced
1 small courgette, sliced
1 carrot, sliced
1 stick celery, chopped
small handful of green beans
250ml/9fl oz vegetable stock *or* water
15ml/1 tablespoon freshly chopped parsley
Freshly grated Parmesan cheese

Heat the oil in a pan. Stir in the rice and vegetables and cook over a low heat for a couple of minutes. Pour in half the stock/water and simmer until it is absorbed. Add the remaining liquid in stages until the stock is absorbed. The whole cooking time will be about 25 minutes. Stir in the parsley. Transfer to a processor/mouli and blend to the desired consistency, or serve as it is for older babies. Cool quickly and portion for freezing. Stir in Parmesan cheese just before serving.

Macaroni (or spaghetti) cheese with mushrooms

25g/1oz wholemeal macaroni *or* spaghetti
55g/2oz mushrooms, sliced
1 level tablespoon plain flour
15ml/1 tablespoon oil
300ml/½ pint vegetable stock *or* skimmed milk
40g/1½oz Cheddar cheese, grated, *plus* an extra 25g/1oz, grated, for serving
25g/1oz wholemeal breadcrumbs

Boil the pasta in plenty of water until *al dente* (cooked, but offering some resistance to the teeth). Drain, then chop the spaghetti. Put the mushrooms in a pan with the flour and oil and stir over a moderate heat to make a thick paste. Gradually stir in the stock or milk, a little at a time, to make a thickened sauce. When all the liquid is added, take off the heat and stir in the cheese and pasta. If serving at once, for older babies sieve/mouli or chop, take a portion and top with breadcrumbs mixed with the remaining cheese and brown either in a pre-heated oven or under the grill. Otherwise cool quickly and portion for freezing.

COOKING TIP
A quantity of breadcrumb and cheese mixture is handy to keep ready-mixed in a polythene bag in the freezer.

Chicken with vegetables and rice

55g/2oz brown rice
1 chicken breast, skinned, boned and sliced
1 courgette, sliced
1 carrot, grated
55g/2oz peas

Wash the rice and cover with 5cm/2in water. Bring to the boil, lower the heat and simmer for 15 minutes. Add the remaining ingredients, cover and simmer for 20 minutes, topping up with boiling water as necessary. Transfer to a blender and process to the desired consistency. Cool quickly and portion for freezing.

Lentils Paysanne

Always wash lentils well in several changes of water. At the same time pick them over and remove any stones or grit. Cooking time will depend on the type of lentils used: split red lentils cook in 15 minutes, green and brown take about 25 minutes.

115g/4oz lentils (green, brown or split red)
1 bay leaf
1 bouquet garni (sprigs of parsley and thyme; optional)
1 large carrot, sliced
2 sticks celery, chopped
4 mushrooms, sliced

Put the washed lentils in a pan with the other ingredients and cover with cold water to a level about 2.5cm/1in above the contents of the pan. Bring to the boil, reduce the heat and simmer gently for 20–35 minutes until the lentils are cooked and the water has been absorbed but without leaving the mixture too dry. Remove the bay leaf and bouquet garni and either transfer to a liquidiser/sieve/mouli, or serve as it is for older babies.

Apricot semolina

There is no added sugar in this recipe. The fruit puree will make it sweet enough.

2 teaspoons semolina
150ml / ¼ pint milk
tiny knob butter (optional)
15ml / 1 tablespoon dried apricot puree (page 115)

Put the semolina into a small milk pan or a jug suitable for use in the microwave. Slowly stir in the milk to make a smooth paste, stirring carefully to avoid lumps forming. Place on the heat and simmer, stirring, until the mixture thickens. Do not let it boil. If using a microwave put the jug in on full power for periods of 30 seconds, whisking or stirring well between each, until the semolina has thickened. Remove from the heat and stir in the apricot puree

COOKING TIP
If you use an ice cube of previously prepared apricot puree the temperature will reduce quickly for serving. Just stir into hot semolina.

Meatballs with tomato sauce and rice

Mince the lamb twice to make it extra fine and soft for your baby.

250g/9oz lean lamb e.g. fillet or steaks
1 medium carrot, finely grated
squeeze of tomato puree
15ml/1 tablespoon chopped fresh parsley
425ml/ ¾ pint passata (sieved tomato sauce)
55g/2oz brown rice

Put the mince in a food processor with the carrot, tomato puree and parsley, mix well, then form into 10 small meatballs. Pour the passata in an ovenproof dish or saucepan and add the meatballs. Either cook on

THE ABC OF HEALTHY EATING FOR BABIES AND TODDLERS

the hob or bake in a pre-heated oven 180°C/350°F/Gas 4 for 25–30 minutes (either method). Meanwhile, wash and steam or boil the rice in twice its volume of water until the water is absorbed and the rice is cooked – approximately 30 minutes. Transfer the meatballs, tomato sauce and rice to the blender and process to the desired consistency, or chop for older babies. Cool quickly and portion for freezing.

Courgette gratin

300ml / ½ pint skimmed milk
1 level tablespoon plain flour
25g/1oz soft margarine
2 courgettes, chopped or sliced
2 tablespoons frozen peas
1 tablespoon chopped fresh parsley
55g / 2oz Cheddar cheese, grated
1 large potato, very thinly sliced

Put the milk, flour and margarine in a pan over a low heat and whisk all the time until you have a thick sauce. Continue cooking and stirring for a couple more minutes, then remove from the heat. Put the courgettes and frozen peas in a microwaveable dish with a lid and cook on full power for 2 minutes, stirring once. Remove, and stir into the white sauce with the parsley and cheese. Arrange the potato slices over the top and bake in a pre-heated oven 190°C/375°F/Gas 5 for 20 minutes, or brush the top lightly with oil and put under a hot grill until the potatoes are cooked. Transfer the finished dish to a mouli/blender and process to the desired consistency, or chop for older babies. Cool quickly and portion for freezing.

Salmon dinner

225g/8oz salmon fillet, skinned and boned
350g/12oz potatoes, peeled
280g/10oz can sweetcorn in water (no added salt or sugar)
85g/3oz peas (shelled weight)
1 courgette, peeled and sliced
1 tablespoon finely chopped fresh parsley

Steam the salmon for 6 minutes and flake into a bowl. Boil the potatoes and mash them roughly. Put the sweetcorn in a blender and puree it, then pass through a mouli/sieve to remove the husks. Steam the peas and the courgettes for 5 minutes. Mix all the ingredients together well, including the parsley, and serve. Cool quickly and portion the remainder for freezing.

Spinach dhal and rice

1 cm/½in root ginger
55g/2oz split red lentils, washed (see spinach puree on page 114 for method)
600ml/1pint water
225g/8oz fresh spinach, washed (see spinach puree recipe)
175g/6oz sweet potato, peeled and chopped
175g/6oz carrots, chopped
1 tablespoon finely chopped fresh coriander

Peel the ginger and chop it small enough to put into a garlic press to extract 1 teaspoon of pulpy juice. Discard the fibrous root. Wash the lentils carefully, put them in a pan with the water, spinach, potato and carrot and simmer for about 25 minutes, until the lentils have absorbed most of the liquid and are cooked. Stir in the ginger juice and coriander and cook for a further 5 minutes. Transfer to a mouli/ blender and process to the desired consistency, or serve as it is for older babies. Cool quickly and portion for freezing.

THE ABC OF HEALTHY EATING FOR BABIES AND TODDLERS

Liver casserole

15ml/1 tablespoon oil

1 leek, washed and sliced

2 carrots, sliced

1 large potato, peeled and chopped

8 mushrooms, sliced

1 apple, peeled and sliced

175g/6oz lamb's liver

plain flour for dusting

450ml/16fl oz vegetable stock *or* water

Heat the oil in a pan and add the vegetables and apple, stirring well. Cover and cook for 5 minutes, stirring occasionally to prevent the food sticking to the base of the pan. Slice the liver and dust with flour. Pour into the pan just enough stock/water to cover the vegetables. Lay the liver slices on top, cover the pan and simmer gently for 20 minutes until the vegetables and liver are cooked. Transfer to a mouli/blender and process to the desired consistency, or chop for older babies. Cool quickly and portion for freezing.

Real fruit jelly

You cannot freeze this recipe, and your baby will not eat it all. So make it on an occasion when other members of the family will be present to eat it. Use any fruit you like except pineapple, which interferes with the setting agent.

½ teaspoon agar-agar *or* Gelozone *or* other vegetable setting agent

100ml/3½ fl oz water

300ml/½ pint orange juice

1 medium mango, peeled and chopped

1 ripe peach, peeled, stoned and chopped

175g/6oz raspberries *or* strawberries

Mix the setting agent to a smooth paste with the cold water. Add the orange juice and bring to the boil in a pan, stirring all the time, to dissolve. Remove from the heat and allow to cool. Mix the fruit and put it in a 24cm/9½in terrine or mould. Pour the cooled jelly over it and pack the fruit down. Refrigerate to allow the jelly to set.

Fresh tomato pasta

15ml/1 tablespoon vegetable oil
1 red pepper, deseeded and chopped
1 carrot, chopped
85g/3oz wholemeal pasta
450g/1lb ripe tomatoes, skinned, deseeded and chopped
150ml/¼ pint vegetable stock *or* water
To serve: freshly grated Parmesan cheese

Heat the oil in a pan and add the pepper and carrots. Cover and cook for 10 minutes, stirring occasionally to prevent sticking. Meanwhile boil the pasta in plenty of water until *al dente* (cooked but offering some resistance to the teeth). Drain. For small babies transfer the pasta to a processor/mouli, for older babies just chop it to a suitable size and put on one side. Add the tomatoes and stock/water to the pepper and carrot mixture and continue cooking for a further 10 minutes, stirring occasionally. For small babies pour the sauce over the pasta in the processor and blend to the desired consistency. For older babies pour the sauce over the pasta. Cool quickly and portion the remainder for freezing. To serve: sprinkle grated Parmesan on top.

THE ABC OF HEALTHY EATING FOR BABIES AND TODDLERS

Tuna risotto

15ml/1 tablespoon oil
55g/2oz arborio rice
1 leek, sliced
2 sticks celery, sliced
400g/14oz can tomatoes
250ml/9fl oz vegetable stock *or* water
200g/7oz can tuna in water, drained and flaked
150g/5½oz can sweetcorn in water (no added salt or sugar)
To serve: freshly grated Parmesan cheese

Heat the oil in a pan, stir in the rice, leek and celery and cook over a low heat for 5 minutes. Add the tomatoes and half the stock/water and simmer until it is absorbed. Add the remaining liquid in stages until the stock is absorbed. The whole cooking time will be about 25 minutes. Five minutes before the end of cooking stir in the tuna and sweetcorn. Transfer to a processor/mouli and blend to the desired consistency, or serve as it is for older babies. Cool quickly and portion for freezing. To serve, stir in the Parmesan cheese.

Salmon pâté

115g/4oz salmon steak
115g/4oz medium fat soft cheese
1 ripe avocado
Crispbread *or* toast *or* rice cake

Poach or grill the salmon and, when cool enough to handle, remove the skin and flake the flesh from the bones into the processor/mouli with the cheese. Blend to a pâté of the desired consistency. For older babies simply use a fork to mix the cheese and salmon to a pâté or sandwich spread/toast topping. Serve with fingers of ripe avocado and the crispbread/toast/rice cake.

Fruit compôte

600ml/1 pint water
½ teaspoon ground cinnamon
½ teaspoon ground nutmeg
strip unwaxed or organic orange peel, blanched*
55g/2oz dried apricots
55g/2oz no-need-to-soak dried peaches
55g/2oz no-need-to-soak prunes
55g/2oz raisins *or* sultanas

Put the water, spices and orange peel in a pan and bring to the boil. Reduce the heat to simmering and add the dried fruit. Cover and simmer for about 25 minutes until the fruit is soft. Top up with more water if necessary. Transfer to a processor/mouli and blend to a puree for babies, or chop the fruit for older babies. Serve with natural or vanilla yogurt.
* To blanch orange peel put it in a basin and pour over boiling water to cover. Leave for three minutes, drain and use.

Minestrone

30ml/2 tablespoons olive oil
1 onion, chopped
2 garlic cloves, crushed (optional)
2 carrots, diced
2 sticks celery, chopped
115g/4oz French beans, sliced
2 courgettes, chopped
450g/1lb tomatoes, chopped, *or* 400g/14oz canned tomatoes
1.2 litres/2 pints chicken stock *or* vegetable stock
2 teaspoons fresh thyme leaves
400g/14oz can cannellini *or* other white beans
55g/2oz macaroni *or* other small pasta shape
4 tablespoons chopped fresh parsley
To serve: Parmesan cheese, grated

THE ABC OF HEALTHY EATING FOR BABIES AND TODDLERS

Heat the oil in a large pan, add the onion and garlic and soften. Add all the vegetables. Stir well. Pour in the stock and add the thyme leaves. Bring to the boil, cover, reduce the heat and simmer for 25 minutes. Drain and rinse the canned beans and stir them in, together with the pasta and parsley. Simmer for 12–15 minutes until the pasta is cooked. Transfer to a processor/mouli and blend to a puree for young babies, or serve as it is for older babies. Cool quickly and portion for freezing. Sprinkle some Parmesan over the minestrone at the table.

SERVING TIP

Allow toddlers to help themselves to Parmesan cheese, but put a small amount in a dish beside their plate so that they can help themselves without taking too much!

Chicken and sweetcorn

1 chicken breast, skinned, boned and cubed
1 carrot, grated
1 potato, chopped
140g/5oz swede, chopped
85g/3oz sweetcorn canned in water (no added salt or sugar)

Put the ingredients in a pan with enough water to cover. Bring to the boil, lower the heat and simmer for 20 minutes. Top up with boiling water, if necessary. Transfer to a blender and process to the desired consistency. Cool quickly and portion for freezing.

Lentil and bean cobbler

The 'cobbler' in this recipe is a delicious savoury scone-like topping.

115g/4oz split red lentils, washed
1 bay leaf
15ml/1 tablespoon oil
1 red pepper, deseeded and chopped
1 stick celery, chopped
425ml/¾ pint carrot juice *or* vegetable juice
400g/14oz can red kidney beans, drained and rinsed

COBBLER
225g/8oz plain flour
1 teaspoon baking powder
55g/2oz butter *or* polyunsaturated margarine
25g/1oz Parmesan cheese, grated
200ml/½ pint milk

Put the lentils and bay leaf in a pan and cover with cold water to a level about 2.5cm/1 in above the lentils. Bring to the boil, reduce the heat and simmer for about 25 minutes until the lentils have absorbed most of the liquid and are cooked.

Pre-heat-the oven to 190°C/375°F/Gas 5. Heat the oil in a pan and sauté the pepper and celery for 10–15 minutes until soft and cooked. Transfer to a processor, add the vegetable juice and puree to a sauce. Transfer to an ovenproof dish and stir in the lentils and beans.

To make the cobblers, sift the flour and baking powder into a bowl and rub in the fat until the mixture resembles breadcrumbs. Stir in the cheese. Make a well in the middle and stir in the milk. Turn on to a floured surface and knead lightly until the dough can be rolled out. Cut out rounds or other shapes and put on top of the dish of lentils and beans in sauce. Bake in the oven for 15 minutes until the cobblers are risen and golden brown.

When cooked, transfer to the blender and process to the desired consistency, or serve as it is for older babies. Cool quickly and portion for freezing.

Spinach and lentil 'pie'

115g/4oz split red lentils, washed
1 bay leaf
115g/4oz frozen spinach, leaf or chopped, thawed,
or 225g/8oz fresh spinach, washed
1 teaspoon ground cumin
150ml/¼ pint passata (sieved tomato sauce)
450g/1lb potatoes, peeled and chopped
30–45ml/2–3 tablespoons milk

Put the lentils and bay leaf in a pan and cover with cold water to a level about 2.5cm/1 in above the lentils. Bring to the boil, reduce the heat and simmer for about 25 minutes, until the lentils have absorbed most of the liquid and are cooked. Remove the bay leaf.

If using fresh spinach, wash and cook (see spinach puree recipe on page 114). Stir the thawed or cooked spinach into the lentils with the cumin and passata. Transfer from the pan to an ovenproof dish.

Boil the potatoes until just cooked, drain and return to the pan with the milk. Mash until smooth. Spoon the mashed potatoes on to the lentil mixture, spreading with a fork to give a rough top. If necessary, put under a pre-heated grill or in the oven to heat through and brown. Transfer to the blender and process to the desired consistency, or serve as it is for older babies. Cool quickly and portion for freezing.

Fruit fool

For a quick fruit fool stir stewed fruit (fresh or dried), fruit compôte or puree (see recipes on pages 111–13) into natural or Greek yogurt or cold custard.

Fish with parsley sauce

White fish goes best with sauce, but salmon is also acceptable to most babies. Choose any fillet, cutlet or steak from which the bones may be easily removed.

1 small fillet *or* portion from larger fillet of e.g. plaice, cod,
halibut, coley – approx 175g/6oz
4 small broccoli florets
4 mushrooms, thinly sliced, *and/or*
15ml/1 tablespoon chopped fresh parsley
1 level tablespoon plain flour
15ml/1 tablespoon oil
300ml/½ pint milk

Poach or grill the fish, then flake from the skin if necessary. Steam or boil the broccoli florets. Put the mushrooms (if using) in a pan with the flour and oil and stir over a moderate heat to make a thick paste. Gradually stir in the milk, a little at a time, to make a sauce. When all the liquid is added, take the pan off the heat and stir in the flaked fish, broccoli and parsley (if using). Transfer to a processor/mouli. Quickly cool what is not being served and portion for freezing. For older babies, pour the sauce over the cooked fish fillet and broccoli, neither of which need be stirred into the sauce.

Baked potato with apple and cheese

The quickest way (15–20 minutes) to produce baked potatoes with a crispy skin is by cooking in a combination oven, (simultaneous microwave and conventional heat). Otherwise scrubbed potatoes will take about 1–1¼ hours in a pre-heated oven at 200°C/400°F/Gas 6.

When cooked, cut in half and mash some milk into the potato flesh to moisten and cool for impatient or hungry babies. Add finely grated apple and Cheddar cheese.

Other baked potato fillings

Carrot and cheese
Yogurt and chives
Smoked salmon (diced) and medium fat soft cheese
Ham (diced) and soft or grated hard cheese
Grated cheese and grape halves
Soft cheese and raisins
Prawn and yogurt with a little tomato ketchup

Meatloaf and potatoes

450g/1lb lean lamb, minced twice
1 large carrot, grated
1 onion, grated
2 teaspoons tomato puree
85g/3oz wholemeal breadcrumbs
1 teaspoon Dijon mustard
150ml/¼ pint passata (sieved tomato sauce)

Pre-heat the oven to 180°C/350°F/Gas 4. Mix the lamb thoroughly with all the ingredients. Turn into a lightly oiled terrine or loaf tin and bake for 1 hour. Remove from the oven and leave to stand for 5 minutes before turning out and slicing. Reserve any cooking liquid to use when mashing the meatloaf for younger babies. Serve with boiled or mashed potatoes and a green vegetable, pureed or chopped as appropriate. Quickly cool what is not being served and portion for freezing.

Frozen vegetable gratin

350g/12oz potatoes, peeled and chopped
30–45ml/2–3 tablespoons milk
450g/1lb pack mixed frozen vegetables
300ml/½ pint boiling water *or* stock
10ml/2 teaspoons cornflour
2 teaspoons tomato puree
85g/3oz Cheddar cheese, grated

Boil the potatoes until just cooked, drain and return to the pan with the milk. Mash until smooth.

Add the vegetables to the boiling water and cook for 5 minutes (or as instructed on the pack). Mix the cornflour to a smooth paste with about a tablespoon of cold water. Stir the tomato puree into the vegetables and add the cornflour paste, stirring over the heat until thickened. Remove from the heat and stir in 55g/2oz of the cheese. Transfer to an ovenproof dish. Spoon the mashed potatoes on to the mixture, spreading with a fork to give a rough top. Sprinkle the remaining cheese over the top and either put under a pre-heated grill or in the oven to heat through and brown.

Transfer to the blender and process to the desired consistency, or serve as it is for older babies. Cool quickly and portion for freezing.

Minced pork with apple sauce

450g/1lb lean pork, minced twice
15ml/1 tablespoon oil
1 red pepper, deseeded and diced
1 eating apple, peeled and sliced
1 carrot, diced
1 small sweet potato, peeled and diced
1 teaspoon chopped fresh sage
10ml/2 teaspoons cornflour
Apple puree (see page 111) as required

Heat the oil in a pan and add the pork and pepper. Mix well and cook for 5 minutes, stirring often. Add all the remaining ingredients except the cornflour and apple puree and mix well. Cover the pan and continue to cook over a low heat for 25 minutes, stirring occasionally to prevent sticking. Mix the cornflour to a smooth paste with about a tablespoon of cold water, then stir into the contents of the pan and gradually add enough boiling water to make the mixture moist and creamy. Transfer to the blender and process to a smoother consistency, if necessary, but if you have diced the vegetables finely it should not need further processing. Pour the apple puree over the dish as you serve it. Cool quickly and portion the remainder for freezing. Serve with vegetables.

Pasta with ricotta

85g/3oz penne (pasta quills)
115g/4oz ricotta *or* medium fat soft cheese
280g/10oz carton/sachet fresh tomato pasta sauce

Boil the pasta in plenty of water until *al dente* (cooked but offering some resistance to the teeth). Drain the pasta, return to the pan, add the ricotta and toss well. Heat the tomato sauce and pour over the cheesy pasta. Transfer to a blender and process to a smoother consistency, or chop for older babies. Cool quickly and portion the remainder for freezing.

Shepherd's pie

350g/12oz potatoes, peeled and chopped
30–45ml/2–3 tablespoons milk
15ml/1 tablespoon oil
450g/1lb lean lamb, minced twice
1 large carrot, grated
1 onion, grated
200ml/½ pint passata (sieved tomato sauce)

Boil the potatoes until just cooked, drain, return to the pan and add the milk. Mash until smooth.

Heat the oil and stir in the lamb, carrot and onion and cook over

a moderate heat for 10 minutes until the vegetables start to soften. Mix in the passata and cook for a further 15 minutes. Pour into a lightly oiled ovenproof dish. Spoon the mashed potatoes on to the mixture, spreading with a fork to give a rough top. Either brown under a pre-heated grill or in a pre-heated oven. Transfer to the blender and process to the desired consistency, or serve as it is for older babies. Cool quickly and portion for freezing.

Cauliflower cheese

Make as for macaroni cheese (page 118), but substitute 175g/6oz steamed or boiled cauliflower florets for the pasta.

Nine to twelve months

Lasagne

8 sheets lasagne

MEAT SAUCE
450g/1lb lean lamb, minced
1 onion, chopped
1 carrot, grated
10ml/2 teaspoons tomato puree
400g/14oz can tomatoes
15ml/1 tablespoon chopped fresh parsley
1 teaspoon chopped fresh thyme

WHITE SAUCE
1 rounded tablespoon plain flour
40g/1½oz margarine
600ml/1 pint milk
85g/3oz Cheddar cheese, grated

THE ABC OF HEALTHY EATING FOR BABIES AND TODDLERS

Boil the lasagne in a large pan of water for 10 minutes, or as directed on the pack (unless using No Pre-Cook lasagne). Drain and rinse in cold water, keeping sheets separate so that they do not stick together.

Preheat the oven to 180°C/350°F/Gas 4. Lightly oil a large ovenproof dish. Put the lamb, onion and carrot into a saucepan and stir over a moderate heat for 10 minutes to brown the meat and slightly soften the vegetables. Stir in the tomato puree, tomatoes and herbs and continue to simmer for a further 10 minutes.

Put the flour and fat in a saucepan and stir over a moderate heat to make a thick paste. Gradually add the milk, stirring well between additions to prevent lumps forming. Take the pan off the heat and stir in the cheese.

To assemble, put a layer of meat sauce in the base, then a layer of lasagne, then a layer of white sauce and so on, finishing with white sauce. Bake in the oven for 30 minutes. Transfer to the blender and process to the desired consistency, or serve as it is for older babies. Cool quickly and portion for freezing.

Spanish omelette

Put some diced cold cooked vegetables such as potatoes, peas or beans in a small frying pan with a knob of butter or vegetable oil and heat through gently. Whisk an egg well and pour it over the vegetables. You may want to contain the vegetable and egg mixture within a small oiled muffin (or similar) ring to give the omelette some shape and depth, as you are using only one egg for your baby. When set, carefully turn the omelette over and cook the other side. Serve with bread.

Mushroom risotto

Follow any of the previous risotto recipes (pages 117 and 125), but substitute one or two types of mushroom for the majority of the vegetables.

Broccoli and tuna pasta

Follow the recipe for pasta with tuna and vegetable sauce (page 116) substituting a head of broccoli florets for the beans and courgette.

Meatloaf II

450g/1lb lean pork, minced
1 small onion, chopped
1 courgette, chopped
1 carrot, grated
1 green pepper, deseeded and chopped
500ml/18 fl oz carton tomato and basil soup
1 teaspoon chopped fresh thyme

Preheat the oven to 190°C/375°F/Gas 5. Put all the ingredients in a food processor and blend finely. Pour into a lightly oiled terrine or loaf tin and bake for 1 hour 10 minutes.

Rice pudding with apricots

Stir some chopped ready-to-eat dried apricots, or fresh sliced apricots, into canned, creamed rice pudding.

Fishcake

115g/4oz mackerel fillet
115g/4oz white fish fillet (e.g. coley, cod)
1 large potato, peeled
600ml/4 tablespoons milk
115g/4oz peas

Put the fish in a saucepan in enough water to cover it and bring to the boil. Reduce heat and simmer for 10 minutes. Drain and flake from

the skin, removing any bones if necessary. Boil the potato, drain and mash with the milk. Boil the peas and drain. Transfer everything to the food processor and blend to the desired consistency, or mash and form into mini-fishcake shapes for older babies. Cool quickly and portion for freezing.

COOKING AND SERVING TIP

Oily fish is such a valuable food (and relatively economical) that it is important to help your baby enjoy it regularly. Mackerel and salmon are the simplest fresh oily fish to prepare for babies as the bones are relatively easily removed (herrings are too bony for babies). My daughter developed a taste for mackerel after first 'accidentally' enjoying grilled mackerel with apple puree and custard! It's worth a try . . .

Ham and pea rosti

Adjust the quantities given here to suit your baby's appetite. Grate a cold cooked potato and mix with 15ml/1 tablespoon cooked peas and a small amount of diced ham. Press lightly into a flat cake shape. Heat 1 teaspoon oil in a non-stick pan and cook on both sides until crisp and golden.

Cheese scone

Use the Fruit Scone recipe in the baking section (page 165), but omit the sugar and raisins and instead add 55–85g/2–3oz grated cheese (the more flavoursome it is, the less you need add). Spread with soft cheese and serve with sticks of carrot and cucumber or pepper.

Lamb shish kebab

Use 40g/1½oz lean lamb per portion. Mince the meat twice and stir in ½ teaspoon tomato puree and 1 teaspoon chopped fresh parsley or a

pinch of thyme. Form around a skewer or satay stick and cook under a pre-heated grill, turning once or twice. Serve with poached mushrooms, plain rice and any other favourite vegetables, whole or pureed.

Cod risotto

Follow the Tuna Risotto recipe on page 125, substituting 250g/9oz cod fillet for the tuna. Add the chopped cod 15 minutes before the end of cooking.

Lamb and bean hotpot

15ml/1 tablespoon oil
175g/6oz neck fillet of lamb, chopped
1 onion, chopped
1 carrot, chopped
2 teaspoons tomato puree
400g/14oz can chopped tomatoes
1 teaspoon chopped fresh oregano *or* marjoram
200g/7oz cooked *or* canned butter beans, sliced

Heat the oil in a pan and lightly brown the lamb with the onion and carrot. Stir in the tomato puree and add the tomatoes and herbs. Either cover and continue to simmer gently on the hob for about 40 minutes, or transfer to a pre-heated moderate oven. Add the beans 15 minutes before the end of the cooking time. Transfer to the food processor and blend to the desired consistency, or mash and form into mini-fishcake shapes for older babies. Cool quickly and portion for freezing.

Avocado risotto

15ml/1 tablespoon oil
1 onion, finely chopped
140g/5oz arborio rice
425ml/¾ pint vegetable stock *or* water
15ml/1 tablespoon finely chopped fresh herbs
(e.g. parsley, basil, chives)
knob butter *or* vegetable margarine
1 avocado, chopped
To serve: freshly grated Parmesan cheese

Heat the oil and gently cook the onion and rice until the rice is opaque. Pour in half the stock/water and simmer until it is absorbed. Add the remaining liquid in stages until it is all absorbed – about 25 minutes. Stir in the herbs, butter/margarine and avocado. Transfer to a processor/mouli and blend to the desired consistency, or serve as it is for older babies. Cool quickly and portion for freezing. Sprinkle the Parmesan over the top just before serving.

Tabbouleh

55g/2oz cracked wheat (bulgur)
¼ cucumber, peeled
¼ green pepper
1 spring onion (optional)
15ml/1 tablespoon fresh chopped mint
Squeeze lemon juice

Boil the cracked wheat for 10 minutes in twice its volume of water and leave to stand for another 10 minutes in order to swell and soften. Squeeze dry, if necessary. Dice the cucumber, pepper and onion very finely and mix in with the cracked wheat, together with the mint and lemon juice.

Pommes Anna with liver

10ml/2 teaspoons oil
1 carrot, chopped
1 stick celery, sliced
400g/14oz can chopped tomatoes
225g/8oz lamb's liver, sliced
450g/1lb potatoes, peeled and thinly sliced
25g/1oz butter, melted

Preheat the oven to 180°C/350°F/Gas 4. Heat the oil in a pan and cook the carrot and celery for 10 minutes until softened. Transfer to an ovenproof dish with the tomatoes and lay the liver on top. Arrange the potato slices on top, overlapping the slices to form a complete seal. Brush with the melted butter and bake for 40 minutes until golden brown. Transfer to a processor/mouli and blend to the desired consistency, or serve as it is for older babies. Cool quickly and portion for freezing.

Potato and watercress soup

1 bunch watercress, washed and trimmed
1 medium potato, chopped
850ml/1½ pints vegetable stock
150ml/¼ pint creamy milk

Put the watercress, potato and stock in a pan and bring to the boil. Cover, and reduce the heat to a simmer for 20 minutes. Transfer to a processor/mouli and blend to the desired consistency. Stir in the milk and return to the pan to heat through. Cool quickly and portion for freezing (you may prefer to freeze the soup without the milk, which can be stirred in before you serve the thawed and reheated portions).

Ratatouille pasta

The Mediterranean vegetable stew called Ratatouille is served in this menu with pasta but it is also a good vegetable accompaniment to meat, fish, quiche and vegetarian main courses. If your baby tolerates garlic well, stir in a couple of crushed cloves 10–15 minutes before the end of cooking – the health benefits of garlic are lost through over-cooking.

30ml/2 tablespoons olive oil
1 onion, sliced
1 aubergine, cubed
1 red pepper, deseeded and cut into strips
1 green pepper, deseeded and cut into strips
2 courgettes, sliced
450g/1lb plum tomatoes, chopped
1 tablespoon freshly chopped mixed herbs
(e.g. basil, parsley, marjoram, oregano, thyme)

Heat the oil in a large heavy-based pan with a well-fitting lid. Add the onion, aubergine and peppers and fry for about 10 minutes over a moderate heat to soften. Add the remaining vegetables and cover the pan to let everything cook in its own steam without the addition of further oil. Transfer to a processor/mouli and blend to the desired consistency. Cool quickly and portion for freezing.

Lean burger

This makes only a couple of portions, or an individual burger for older babies/children.

55g/2oz extra-lean meat
(e.g. lamb/pork/chicken/venison), minced twice
½ carrot, grated
½ tablespoon breadcrumbs
A little passata (sieved tomato sauce) *or* tomato ketchup

Mix the solid ingredients together to form a burger shape, adding passata or ketchup, if needed, to moisten. Either fry in a non-stick pan without added fat, or grill well on both sides. Transfer to a processor/mouli and blend to the desired consistency with a vegetable, for example mashed potato.

Cod in parsley sauce

2 × 150g/5½oz cod steaks
Olive oil
25g/1oz butter
1 tablespoon plain flour
300ml/½ pint milk
Pinch lemon zest (grated rind)
2 tablespoons chopped fresh parsley

Brush the cod steaks with olive oil and grill for about 10 minutes, turning once. Melt the fat in a pan with the flour, stirring it continuously to make a roux (paste). Gradually stir in the milk to make a smooth sauce. Stir in the lemon zest and parsley. Flake the fish from the central bone, being careful to remove all the bones, and pour some of the sauce over it. Serve with boiled potatoes and peas. Transfer the remainder to a processor/mouli and blend to the desired consistency. Serve with vegetables.

Sweetcorn and cheese fritters

Makes about 10 small fritters

115g/4oz wholemeal flour
1 free-range egg
150ml/¼ pint milk
55g/2oz Cheddar *or* Parmesan cheese, grated
115g/4oz sweetcorn, canned in water (no added salt or sugar)
oil for frying

Sift the flour into a bowl, adding the bran left in the sieve. Break the egg into a well in the flour and add a little milk. Gradually whisk the liquid into the flour. When all the milk has been added, stir in the cheese and sweetcorn. Heat a little oil in a non-stick pan and add a couple of tablespoons of the mixture. Cook until both sides are golden brown. Remove excess oil on kitchen paper before serving.

Fishballs with rice and tomato sauce

Follow the recipe for Meatballs with tomato sauce and rice (page 120), but substitute fishballs for meatballs. To make fishballs put the following ingredients in a food processor, blend to a smooth paste and form the mixture into small balls.

375g/13oz mackerel fillets, skinned

250g/9oz coley fillets, skinned

1 garlic clove, crushed (optional)

1 onion, chopped

¼ teaspoon ground cumin

¼ teaspoon ground coriander

2 teaspoons tomato puree

Fish kebabs

The fishball mixture above can also be formed around skewers to make a fish kebab. Cook as for Lamb Shish kebab on page 137.

Cheese polenta with tomato sauce

For variety, on occasion add sweetcorn to the polenta mixture.

140g/5oz polenta (yellow cornmeal)
250ml/9fl oz cold water
450ml/16fl oz chicken stock *or* vegetable stock
6 tablespoons grated Parmesan cheese
To serve: fresh tomatoes *or* cheese, *and* passata (sieved tomato sauce)

Blend the polenta and water in a bowl, using a fork. Bring the stock to the boil in a pan and add the polenta all in one go. Stir until the mixture begins to boil and thicken. Reduce the heat and cook for 10 minutes, stirring all the time to prevent sticking. Remove from the heat and stir in the cheese. Spoon into a lightly oiled cake tin and smooth the top. Leave to set and cool, then slice as much as you need for a serving, top with sliced tomatoes or thinly pared cheese and warm under the grill. Serve with passata or a tomato sauce from a previous recipe. You can store the remainder of the polenta in the fridge for a few days, or else cut into slices and freeze.

Baked potato pizza

Top half a baked potato with either diced bacon or wafer-thin ham, thin slices of Mozzarella or other cheese, and grated carrot (or your baby's favourite vegetable). Pop under the grill until the cheese has melted. Allow to cool before serving, or else transfer to a processor/ mouli and blend to the preferred consistency.

Pasta with poached salmon and soft cheese

Grill or poach a salmon steak, then flake the fish away from the bones and skin. Cook about 115–140g/4–5oz pasta such as tagliatelle. Drain, then toss in a few tablespoons of soft white cheese. Stir in the salmon. Chop, or else transfer to a processor/mouli and blend to the preferred consistency.

Apple sponge

This can be made in individual (double) portions in small ramekins or foil containers specifically for use in the freezer, or in a standard (family) size before being portioned and frozen. Using eating apples avoids the need to add sugar to cooking apples.

450g/1lb dessert apples (e.g. Golden Delicious)
115g/4oz butter *or* margarine
85g/3oz sugar
1 free-range egg, lightly beaten
115g/4oz self-raising flour, sifted

Pre-heat the oven to 180°C/350°F/Gas 4. Peel, core and slice the apples. Put them in a saucepan with a few tablespoons water and cook lightly for 10 minutes, stirring to ensure even cooking. Transfer to an ovenproof baking dish or individual dishes. Cream the fat and sugar until soft, lightly beat in the egg and then fold in the flour. Spoon the sponge mixture over the partially cooked apples and bake for 15–30 minutes, depending on the size of the container(s), or until a skewer inserted into the sponge comes out clean.

Potato parmigiana

450g/1lb new potatoes, scrubbed and sliced
1 aubergine, sliced
30ml/2 tablespoons olive oil
400g/14oz can tomatoes
1 teaspoon tomato puree
1 tablespoon chopped fresh basil
2 tablespoons grated Parmesan cheese
125g/4½oz reduced fat Mozzarella cheese

Pre-heat the oven to 180°C/350°F/Gas 4. Cook the potatoes until tender, then slice then. Brush the aubergine slices with the oil and

grill for 2 minutes each side until lightly golden. Blend the tomatoes, tomato puree and basil to a sauce. Arrange layers of aubergine, Parmesan, potato and tomato sauce in an ovenproof dish, finishing with tomato sauce. Top with the Mozzarella and bake for 25 minutes, until the cheese is browned. Chop, or else transfer to a processor/mouli and blend to the preferred consistency.

One to two years

Mackerel salad

You can use cold cooked fish and potato, or freshly cooked, warm ingredients for this salad.

½ cooked mackerel fillet
1 medium cooked potato
broccoli florets
red-skinned apple, diced

Mix all the ingredients with 1 teaspoon low fat mayonnaise.

Raisin bread and butter pudding

4 slices raisin bread, buttered
25g/1oz raisins *or* currants
1 free-range egg
1 free-range egg yolk
25g/1oz light muscovado sugar
½ teaspoon ground cinnamon (if there is not already cinnamon in the bread)
450ml/16fl oz full fat milk

Cut the slices of bread into halves or quarters and arrange on top of the dried fruit in an ovenproof dish, buttered side up. Whisk the eggs, sugar, cinnamon and milk in a bowl and pour this liquid over the bread. Leave to stand for 30 minutes. Pre-heated the oven to 180°C/350°F/Gas 4 and bake until the top is golden brown and the custard is set.

Salmon quiche

This recipe is equally good with Finnan (smoked) haddock. If you do not want to make your own pastry use 175g/6oz ready-made shortcrust pastry.

115g/4oz plain flour
55g/2oz butter *or* margarine
300g/10½oz salmon fillet
150ml/¼ pint single cream *or* full fat milk
2 free-range eggs
1 tablespoon chopped parsley
black pepper (optional)

Pre-heat the oven to 200°C/400°F/Gas 6. Sift the flour into a mixing bowl and rub in the fat until the mixture resembles breadcrumbs. Gradually stir in cold water to make a soft dough. Roll out on a lightly floured board and line an oiled 20cm/8in flan tin. Line the pastry case with greaseproof paper and baking beans, and bake blind for 10 minutes.

Grill the salmon or poach in enough water to cover it for about 10 minutes or until the fish is cooked. When cool enough to handle, flake the flesh into the base of the pastry case. Beat the cream/milk, eggs, parsley and pepper and pour this mixture over the fish. Lower the oven heat to 190°C/375°F/Gas 5 and bake the flan for 25 minutes. When golden brown and set, remove from the oven and cool on a wire baking tray.

Stir fry chicken

The sauce for this dish contains small amounts of sugar and soy sauce.

1 skinless chicken breast, shredded
30ml/2 tablespoons vegetable oil
2 carrots cut into matchsticks
Handful of broccoli florets
1 red *or* green pepper, deseeded and cut into strips
Handful of mangetout, trimmed
1 courgette, sliced
4 Chinese leaves, shredded

SAUCE
30ml/2 tablespoons soy sauce
125ml/4fl oz orange juice
1 teaspoon tomato puree
15ml/1 tablespoon white wine vinegar
1 tablespoon demerara sugar
2 teaspoons cornflour

Heat the oil in a wok or suitable pan and fry the chicken and vegetables (add the hardest first as it will take longer to cook) to the consistency to suit your baby. Make sure the chicken is cooked thoroughly. Heat all the sauce ingredients except the cornflour in a pan until the sugar has dissolved. Mix the cornflour to a smooth paste with a little cold water, stir the paste into the sauce and cook until thickened. Thin to the preferred consistency by adding boiled water. Pour the sauce over the vegetables and chicken and heat through. Transfer to a blender and process to the desired consistency, or serve as it is for older babies. Cool quickly and portion for freezing. Serve with boiled/steamed brown rice.

Home-made pizza

The amount of water needed to mix the pizza dough will vary according to the flour used, so add cautiously. With practice you will be able to tell by the feel of the dough how much water is needed.

15g/½oz fresh yeast *or* 1 teaspoon dried yeast
200ml/7fl oz lukewarm water
85g/3oz plain unbleached flour
85g/3oz plain wholemeal flour

Dissolve the yeast in the water. Sift the flours into a bowl and make a well in the centre. Pour the yeast mixture into the well and mix to a soft dough. Turn out and knead on a lightly floured surface for 3–5 minutes. Return the dough to the bowl, cover and leave to prove (double in size) in a warm place for 40 minutes (or overnight/during the day in the fridge). Proving can be speeded up with a microwave. Put the covered dough in a suitable container and microwave on full power for 10 seconds, rest for 5 minutes and repeat.

Pre-heat the oven to 200–220°C/400–425°F/Gas 6–7. Knead the dough again for 3 minutes, roll out into a large circle or small (individual) pizzas, and place on a lightly oiled baking sheet. Spread the pizzas with a thin layer of tomato puree with chopped herbs (optional), then add the topping of your choice. Babies like it simple to start with, e.g. grated carrot on top of the puree, topped with a little cheese. As they become familiar with pizzas add more vegetables and other ingredients. Bake for 10–15 minutes until the cheese is brown and the crust crisp.

PIZZA TOPPINGS

Jars or cartons of pizza topping
Sliced tomatoes
Diced bacon or ham
Mashed sardines or other fish
Prawns
Onion

- Courgettes
- Grated carrot
- Peppers
- Slices of sausage
- Top the topping with slices of Mozzarella or other cheese, if liked

Prawn and potato curry

1cm/½ in root ginger

15ml/1 tablespoon oil

1 onion, diced

1 clove garlic, crushed

1 teaspoon mild curry paste

280g/10oz new potatoes, scrubbed and sliced

250g/9oz cooked, peeled prawns

1 tablespoon chopped coriander

Peel the ginger and chop small enough to put into a garlic press to extract 1 teaspoon pulpy juice. Discard the fibrous root. Heat the oil in a pan, add the onion, garlic, ginger juice and curry paste, and cook gently until the onion has softened. Add the potatoes and just enough water to cover them. Bring to the boil, simmer and cook for 10 minutes. Stir in the prawns and simmer for a further 5 minutes, adding more water if needed. Stir in the coriander and serve.

Red pepper soup

15ml/1 tablespoon olive oil

1 onion, diced

1 red pepper, deseeded and chopped

400g/14 oz can tomatoes

300ml/½ pint vegetable stock

Heat the oil and cook the onion and red pepper until softened. Add the tomatoes and continue cooking, stirring occasionally, for 10

THE ABC OF HEALTHY EATING FOR BABIES AND TODDLERS

minutes. Remove the pan from the heat, transfer the mixture and stock to a processor/mouli and puree until smooth. Return the soup to the pan and reheat.

Cod steak with crumb topping

To make a crumb topping for a fish steak, mix breadcrumbs with grated cheese and any of the following optional additions to suit your baby's taste: finely diced sundried tomatoes, a small amount of pesto, fresh or dried herbs of choice. Put the crumb topping on the steak and either grill or bake in the usual way. Serve with vegetable(s).

Frittata

This is a type of omelette filled with vegetables, cooked slowly until set, then served cut into wedges. Small slices can be cut for your baby, who can eat it with his or her fingers. Share the recipe with the rest of the family, as it does not freeze well. Add diced ham, bacon, anchovies, cheese, chicken, tuna and so on to suit your baby's taste or the occasion.

30ml/2 tablespoons olive oil

1 onion, diced

1 red pepper, deseeded and chopped

1 medium courgette, sliced

1 clove garlic, crushed

175g/6oz sweetcorn, canned in water (no added salt or sugar)

2 tomatoes, skinned, deseeded and chopped

2 tablespoons fresh chopped mixed herbs (e.g. basil, parsley, tarragon, chervil)

5–6 free-range eggs, lightly beaten

Heat the oil in a pan and sauté the onion, pepper and courgette until they start to soften. Stir in the garlic, sweetcorn, tomato and herbs. Stir the eggs into the pan and move gently from side to side as the mixture begins to set, so that the runny egg in the middle trickles out

to the side to be cooked. Reduce the heat, cover and cook gently for about 15 minutes until the egg is completely cooked. Invert on to a warmed serving dish.

Spoonable milkshake puddings

These milkshakes make up to 600ml/1pint, so other members of the family will have to share them with your baby (or else just scale down the recipes). Add more milk to enable older children and adults to drink the milkshakes. Put all the ingredients in a blender and blend until smooth.

STRAWBERRY
1 carton strawberry yogurt
1 scoop vanilla frozen yogurt (lower fat than ice cream)
Scant 300ml/½ pint semi-skimmed milk

BANANA AND CUSTARD
150ml/¼ pint low fat ready-to-serve custard
1 banana, peeled and chopped
Scant 300ml/½ pint semi-skimmed milk

PEACHES AND 'CREAM'
2 ripe peaches *or* nectarines
150ml/¼ pint low fat ready-to-serve custard
1 scoop vanilla frozen yogurt (lower fat than ice cream)

Gnocchi in tomato sauce

As a short cut, instead of using the tomato sauce recipe below substitute a 300g/10½oz carton of ready-made plain/fresh tomato sauce or passata (sieved tomato sauce).

15ml/1 tablespoon olive oil

1 medium onion, diced

1 clove garlic, crushed

400g/14 oz tomatoes

1 tablespoon tomato puree

1 tablespoon freshly chopped herbs (parsley, basil, thyme)

GNOCCHI

600ml/1 pint milk

175g/6oz semolina

25g/1oz butter

85g/3oz Parmesan cheese, finely grated

Freshly grated nutmeg

2 free-range eggs

175g/6oz spinach, thawed, with excess moisture pressed out

To make the tomato sauce, first heat the oil in a pan. Add the onion and garlic and cook until translucent. Stir in the remaining ingredients and cook for 20 minutes.

To make the gnocchi, first pre-heat the oven to 190°C/375°F/Gas 5. Heat the milk in a large pan. When it is on the point of boiling slowly pour in the semolina, stirring until smooth and thick, which will take about 2 minutes of continuous cooking and stirring. Remove from the heat and beat in the butter, cheese and nutmeg. Cool slightly for a couple of minutes, then beat in the eggs and spinach. Using a pair of table-spoons, form the mixture into balls and place them in a lightly oiled ovenproof dish big enough to accommodate both gnocchi and sauce. Pour the sauce over the top. Bake in the oven for about 25 minutes.

Lamb with squash and lentils

175g/6oz neck fillet of lamb, chopped
225g/8oz pumpkin *or* other squash, cubed
1 large carrot, chopped
55g/2oz lentils, washed and picked over
1 teaspoon tomato puree
400g/14 oz can tomatoes

Put all the ingredients in a casserole or heavy-based saucepan with a well-fitting lid. Cover with cold water to a level about 5cm/2in above the contents. Bring to the boil, lower the heat and simmer (or bake in a pre-heated moderate oven) for 40 minutes. Serve with green vegetable(s). Transfer to processor/mouli and blend to the desired consistency – with or without serving vegetables. Also suitable for younger babies, if serving them.

Potato and apple pancakes

These pancakes are sweet, but you can omit the apple and raisins and add cheese or serve topped with ham.

225g/8oz potatoes, peeled and chopped
30ml/2 tablespoons milk
25g/1oz plain flour
2 free-range eggs
1 apple, peeled and grated
1 tablespoon raisins
Oil for cooking

Boil the potatoes, drain them and mash with the milk. Leave until cool. Beat the flour and eggs into the mashed potato and stir in the apple and raisins. Heat a little oil in a non-stick pan and add tablespoons of the mixture. Flatten slightly and cook for a couple of minutes each side.

THE ABC OF HEALTHY EATING FOR BABIES AND TODDLERS

Apple crumble

Use the following crumble mixture to top any combination of fresh or dried fruit and bake in a moderate oven (200°C/400°F/Gas 6) for 25 minutes, until the crumble topping is cooked and lightly browned. The crumble mixture can be made in larger batches and stored in the freezer. This allows smaller amounts to be withdrawn as required, for example to top individual baby/child size ramekins of stewed fruit. Serve with natural yogurt or low fat custard.

85g/3oz plain flour
25g/1oz rolled oats
85g/3oz butter *or* margarine
30–45ml/2–3 tablespoons demerara sugar

Rub the fat into the flour until the mixture resembles breadcrumbs in consistency. Stir in the oats and sugar and use as required.

Roast fish and vegetables

45ml/3 tablespoons olive oil
Juice of ½ lemon
2 cloves garlic, crushed (optional)
1 teaspoon wholegrain mustard
1 teaspoon honey
1 red pepper, deseeded and chopped
2 courgettes, cut into chunks
300g/10½oz new potatoes, quartered
1 red onion, cut into chunks
4 tomatoes, quartered
450g/1lb white fish (e.g. cod), skinned and cut into chunks

Pre-heat the oven to 200°C/400°F/Gas 6. Mix the oil, lemon juice, garlic, mustard and honey and put in a roasting pan in the oven. When hot, add the vegetables and toss thoroughly in the oil. Return to the

oven and roast for 30 minutes, stirring a couple of times during cooking. Add the fish and mix well. Continue to cook for a further 10–15 minutes until the fish is cooked. Transfer to a processor/mouli, check for fish bones and blend to the desired consistency.

Two to three years

Chicken in peanut sauce

Younger babies (without peanut allergies) also enjoy this dish. If you are making it for this age group transfer the cooked dish to a processor/mouli and puree in the usual way.

15ml/1 tablespoon oil
1 large onion, diced
1 teaspoon fresh ginger juice (see page 122)
2 chicken breasts, skinned and cubed
450g/1lb tomatoes, canned *or* fresh, chopped
200g/7oz crunchy peanut butter
1 aubergine, chopped
115g/4oz okra, washed and stems cut off
To serve: diced mango and banana

Heat the oil in a heavy-based pan, add the onion and ginger and cook gently for 5 minutes. Stir in the chicken, tomatoes and peanut butter and simmer for 20 minutes. Meanwhile steam or boil the aubergine and okra for 10 minutes. Drain and add to the chicken mixture. Cover and cook over a low to moderate heat for a further 10 minutes. Serve with the mango and banana 'salad' and plain brown rice.

COOKING TIP
Quick peanut sauce. Stir peanut butter over a moderate heat with passata to desired consistency.

Mango hedgehog

Cut a mango in half, slicing as close to the pip as possible. Put the half on a chopping board and cut through the flesh to the skin at 1cm/½in intervals. Turn the half and cut the opposite way to produce squares. Push the base of the skin upwards to make a 'hedgehog'.

Real fruit brûlée

Put a portion of stewed or fresh fruit of your baby's choice into an individual serving dish. Top with natural (standard or Greek) yogurt and sprinkle a little demerara sugar over the top. Put under a pre-heated grill until the sugar melts and bubbles. Cool slightly before serving.

Quick meals and snacks for two- to three-year-olds

Carrot and peanut butter salad

If your child likes peanut butter, stir a little into grated raw carrots or other vegetables to make a simple salad.

Coleslaw

Toddlers often like this salad if you include a higher ratio of grated carrot to white cabbage and stir in some chopped apple, diced dates and raisins. Mix with a little low fat mayonnaise or natural yogurt.

Stuffed dates

Remove the stones from standard fresh or Medjool dates and fill with low or medium fat soft white cheese.

Leek and cheese rosti

Grate 1 medium potato (cooked or raw), ½ leek and 15g/½oz tasty cheese such as mature Cheddar or Parmesan. Squeeze excess water from the raw potato. Mix the ingredients together. Heat a little oil in a non-stick pan and press the potato mixture into a cake shape in it. Cook for 4 minutes on either side.

Felafels

400g/14oz can chickpeas
1 garlic clove (optional)
½ red pepper, deseeded and chopped
1 teaspoon ground coriander
1 tablespoon chopped fresh parsley

Put all the ingredients in a processor and blend to a fine paste. Roll into small balls and bake in a pre-heated oven at 180°C/350°F/Gas 4 for 20 minutes or deep fry in oil for 5 minutes. Drain on absorbent kitchen paper and cool before serving.

Chinese prawn toast

Mash 55g/2oz peeled cooked prawns with a squeeze of lemon juice and 15ml/1 tablespoon low fat mayonnaise. Cut the crusts off 2 slices wholemeal bread and toast one side of each slice. Spread the untoasted side with the prawns and gently press some sesame seeds on top. Pop under the grill until the seeds are golden and the prawns heated through, or put them in a moderate oven for 10–15 minutes.

Romy's mashed prawns

Simply mash prawns with a little lemon juice and, if you like, finely chopped parsley. Serve on bread or with wholewheat crackers.

Popcorn

This is a great snack that toddlers can watch or 'help' prepare. Put a couple of handfuls of popping corn in a pan with a well-fitting lid. Add 15ml/1 tablespoon oil, put the lid on and place the pan over a moderate heat. Soon you will hear a popping noise as the corn 'explodes' and hits the lid of the pan. Turn down the heat. Shake the pan occasionally until the popping stops. Remove the lid carefully so that you or your child are not hit in the eye by flying popcorn. When cool enough to handle, eat as it is, drizzle a small amount of clear honey over it, or stir in a tablespoon of peanut butter (warmed slightly in the microwave to make it more pliable) or a teaspoon of Marmite.

Other useful snacks or meals

- Boiled egg with Marmite soldiers
- Raisin bread, toasted and topped with soft cheese and grape halves
- Rice cakes
- Crispbread
- Breadsticks (grissini)
- Twiglets
- Crisps (unsalted, such as Smith's Salt 'N' Shake)

SNACK TIP

Never give toddlers a whole packet of crisps. Get into the habit of serving crisps and other savoury snacks in a very small dish or bowl. This not only makes more of an 'occasion' of these high fat and high salt foods (if you are not buying reduced fat and no-sugar crisps), but it also allows you to control the portion size without asking the impossible of a toddler – to eat only half a bag of crisps!

Useful convenience foods

Filled pasta

These are pasta shapes such as tortellini, filled with meat, fish, cheese or vegetables. Add to the saucepan of cooking pasta some sliced carrots, beans, or courgettes or other vegetable. Serve with ready-made pasta sauces e.g. fresh tomato, vegetable or tomato and Mascarpone. Offer grated cheese, in addition, if the sauce is not already rich.

Garlic bread

Offer shop garlic bread (some taste reasonable), or focaccia containing olives or sun-dried tomatoes, with soup.

Fresh soup

Add to purchased cartons and sachets more vegetables if necessary, or slivers of cooked chicken, or top with grated cheese as appropriate. Serve with crusty bread or toast.

Crispbread and dips

For dips use soft cheese and herb, or soft cheese and tuna, or tzatziki, or taramasalata.

Muesli

This is good at any time of day. Stir in fresh or dried fruit.

Quiche

Quite high calorie, but you can buy some very tasty ones. Serve hot or cold with vegetables.

HOME-MADE QUICHE FILLING IDEAS

- Ratatouille
- Spinach and lentils
- Spinach and ham
- Bacon and cauliflower
- Mushrooms
- Tuna and sweetcorn

Pizza and salad

Add extra vegetables to bought pizzas. The main elements such as ham or tomato rings or cheese can be lifted up and grated fresh/ blanched vegetables inserted to make a substantial meal.

Sandwiches

These make an ideal meal at any time of day. If you are doing the supermarket shopping with a toddler in tow, offer a sandwich as your child sits in the trolley rather than confectionery or crisps.

SANDWICH FILLINGS

- Soft cheese and Marmite
- Diced beetroot and rollmop herring in low fat mayonnaise or cheese
- Grated cheese and grated carrot or diced apple
- Soft cheese with diced celery
- Tuna or other canned fish mixed with soft cheese and diced cucumber
- Hummus and grated carrot

- Avocado (mashed or sliced) with ham or bacon and tomato
- Egg and chopped watercress

Mash peanut butter with one of the following:
- Mashed banana
- Grated apple
- Grated carrot
- Banana also mashes well with soft cheese

SERVING SANDWICHES

At home always add a garnish of fresh fruit or vegetables which you expect to be eaten. Choose from slices of apples, pears, halved grapes, apricot halves, berry fruits, grated carrot or carrot sticks, cress, raisins, chopped watercress, celery sticks and so on.

TOAST TOPPINGS

- Baked beans
- Sardines
- Pilchards
- Spinach and goat's or soft cheese (not for children under 3 years)
- Ham and pineapple
- Scrambled egg
- Marmite
- Cheese and ham
- Chopped chicken in mango chutney

Chocolate cup 'o' tea

Dissolve ¼ teaspoon (use a Calpol spoon to measure!) cocoa in boiling water, stir in milk to taste and serve hot or cold. As toddlers get older you may need to add ½ teaspoon honey to make the drink more palatable.

Ice cream or frozen yogurt

Do not serve on its own. Make it clear from the start that ice cream is eaten with fresh fruit such as fresh fruit salad, orange segments, strawberries, raspberries and so on. No fruit – no ice cream.

Kebabs

These are quick to cook under the grill or on a barbecue. Children love them, but remove the food from the sticks after putting the kebabs on their plate. Dispose of the sticks so that they cannot poke them into eyes or use them as weapons.

SOME TASTY KEBAB COMBINATIONS
- Lamb with cherry tomatoes
- Courgettes, mushrooms and peppers
- Ham wrapped round monkfish pieces with vegetables
- Bacon wrapped round Mozzarella cheese with pineapple chunks
- Chicken satay pieces with vegetables
- Sausages with cherry tomatoes and other vegetables

Healthy home-made oven chips

As tasty as normal chips, with a fraction of the fat. Peel potatoes and cut into chips in the usual way. Boil the chips in water or stock (use Marmite stock cube) for about 5 minutes until just tender. Drain and cool. (Freeze well at this stage, cook later from frozen.) Toss chips in a polythene bag containing one to two tablespoonsful of fat. Remove to a baking tray and cook in a pre-heated oven at 200°C/ 400°F/Gas 6 for 10 to 15 minutes, turning once.

Nutritious bakes and treats

Toddlers as young as two will love to 'help' make the following recipes. Be prepared for them to dip their fingers in the mixtures (beware those containing raw egg), measure out the dried fruit (mainly into their mouths), knead pastry or bread/pizza dough (to

an unrecognisable grey lump), and feel the texture of the ingredients. Give them their own small bowl, spoon, biscuit cutter and so on on a tray to catch the mess and drips. And have fun. Yum yum . . .

Oatcakes

Makes about 20. Store in an airtight tin when cold.

> 225g/8oz medium oatmeal
> 55g/2oz wholemeal flour
> 1 teaspoon baking powder
> 55g/2oz butter *or* polyunsaturated margarine
> Boiling water to mix

Pre-heat the oven to 190°C/375°F/Gas 5. Mix the dry ingredients. Melt the fat and stir it in. Gradually add enough boiling water to make a soft dough. Knead lightly on a floured surface, then roll out and cut into triangles. Carefully lift on to a lightly oiled baking tray, sprinkle with a little more oatmeal and bake for 10–15 minutes. Do not let the oatcakes get too highly coloured. Cool on a wire rack.

Granny Pa's oatmeal biscuits

Makes about 25. Store in an airtight tin when cold.

> 200g/7oz medium oatmeal
> 150g/5½oz wholemeal flour
> 55g/2oz demerara sugar
> 1 teaspoon baking powder
> 115g/4oz unsalted butter
> 1 free-range egg
> Few tablespoons milk

Pre-heat the oven to 190°C/375°F/Gas 5. Mix the dry ingredients and rub in the fat to make a breadcrumb consistency. Make a well in the middle and pour the beaten egg and milk into it. Mix to a stiffish dough. Lightly knead on a floured surface, then roll out thinly and cut out

THE ABC OF HEALTHY EATING FOR BABIES AND TODDLERS

biscuits with a cutter. Carefully lift on to a lightly oiled baking tray and brush with milk or beaten egg. Bake for 15 minutes until golden brown.

Fruit scones

Makes 8 scones, or 12 if you use a small cutter. They are best eaten on the day they are baked, but will freeze well. Other dried fruit, e.g. sultanas, naturally coloured cherries, finely chopped dried apricots, peaches or dates, also work well.

225g/8oz flour, half and half wholemeal *and* unbleached white
1 teaspoon baking powder
55g/2oz butter *or* polyunsaturated margarine
40g/1½oz light muscovado sugar
55g/2oz raisins
150ml/¼ pint buttermilk *or* milk with a few drops of lemon juice to sour it
Milk to glaze

Pre-heat the oven to 225°C/425°F/Gas 7. Sift the flour and baking powder into a bowl. Rub in the fat to resemble breadcrumbs. Stir in the sugar and raisins. Make a well in the middle and gradually stir in the milk to form a soft dough. Turn the dough on to a lightly floured board and gently knead until it can be rolled to the thickness of your choice. Cut out the scones with a cutter, put on a lightly oiled baking tray and brush with milk. Bake for 10–15 minutes.

Carrot cake

2 free-range eggs
115g/4oz dark muscovado sugar
85ml/3fl oz sunflower oil
175g/6oz grated carrot
115g/4oz wholemeal flour
1 teaspoon baking powder
1 teaspoon ground cinnamon
½ teaspoon ground nutmeg
55g/2oz walnut pieces
55g/2oz raisins

55g/2oz unsalted butter

55g/2oz icing sugar

15ml/1 tablespoon clear honey

Few drops sweet orange oil

Pre-heat the oven to 190°C/375°F Gas 5. Whisk the eggs and sugar until thick and creamy. Whisk in the oil. Using a metal tablespoon, carefully fold in the rest of the ingredients, working as quickly as possible. Pour into a lightly oiled 18cm/7in cake tin. Bake for about 30 minutes or until an inserted skewer comes out clean.

To make the frosting, beat all the ingredients together and cover the cake when it is completely cold.

Fruity rice pudding

850ml/1½ pints milk

4 whole green cardamoms

½ cinnamon stick

85g/3oz pudding (short grain) rice

25g/1oz muscovado sugar

55g/2oz currants

55g/2oz raisins

4 dried apricots, chopped

Freshly grated nutmeg

25g/1oz unsalted butter

Put the milk, cardamoms and cinnamon stick by in a pan and heat gently for 10 minutes. Remove the spices and add the washed rice. Simmer gently for 20 minutes, stirring often. Pre-heat the oven to 180°C/350°F/Gas 4. Transfer to a ½litre/2pint ovenproof dish. Stir in the sugar and fruit and bake for 30 minutes. Remove from the oven, sprinkle the nutmeg over the top and dot with the butter. Return to the oven for 15 minutes for a golden brown pudding.

THE ABC OF HEALTHY EATING FOR BABIES AND TODDLERS

As a short cut, open a can of creamed rice pudding and stir in some raisins. Serve cold, or warm through.

Blackberry and apple summer pudding

Individual puddings made in ramekins will freeze well.

2 eating apples, peeled, cored and cut into chunks
225g/8oz blackberries
8 slices bread from a medium sandwich loaf, crusts removed

Invert a 850ml/1½ pint pudding basin on greaseproof paper and draw round it. Cut out a circle of paper that fits just inside the rim. Put the fruit and 4 tablespoons water into a pan, cover and cook over a gentle heat for 10 minutes until the apples are just cooked, but not mushy. Line the base and sides of the basin with 6 slices of the bread, cutting and trimming as necessary so that no gaps are left. Transfer the fruit and juice to the lined pudding basin. Top with the remaining slices of bread. Cover the basin with the greaseproof paper circle. Put a saucer on top and weigh it down with a heavy can so that the fruit juice will soak into the bread. When cold, transfer to the fridge and chill for at least 2 hours. To serve, remove the weight and unmould the pudding on to a plate.

CHAPTER 5

Food scares

Parent Action on everything from patulin in apple juice to BSE, salmonella, pesticides, sex hormones in soya formula and so on . . .

When a food scare hits the headlines parents have to judge quickly whether the issue will affect the health of their child, and whether they need to act on it. For example, should you have switched brands of artificial baby milk over the 'sex-change' scares linked to soya milk and phthalates in formula? Should you avoid beef when weaning your baby because of the risk of BSE? Should you stop eating nuts if you are breastfeeding to avoid potentially life-threatening allergies in your baby?

If only there were easy answers to these scares – and those yet to come. Cynical readers will believe that the risks are over-stated and that the gullible are being alarmed unnecessarily just to sell a few more newspapers. Concerned readers will be convinced that it is only the tip of the iceberg and that the dangers are even greater than stated by the experts.

You may try to seek help from a health professional. But the chances are that they will not have much more information than you have already gleaned from the media. Or they may be put in the

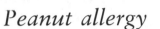

invidious position of passing on platitudes prepared by their managers.

In the end, the buck stops with parents. This chapter may help you make up your mind about current issues and provide some helpful guidelines when weighing up the pros and cons of future issues.

Peanut allergy

Recent research has revealed a rise in potentially life-threatening peanut allergies among babies and children in both Britain and America. Twenty per cent of children will suffer from some form of allergy at some time, and 1 in 200 could have reactions to peanuts and tree nuts by the age of four.

No one knows why more babies and young children are becoming allergic to peanuts, and at an earlier age (before two years), but there are probably two main reasons. Firstly, peanuts and peanut products are introduced into the diet earlier than before, partly because they are more widely used and given to babies unwittingly. Secondly, there is a general increase in allergic disease in the population. This means that there are more people, including a greater proportion of babies and young children, with asthma, allergic rhinitis (runny nose), hay fever and allergy-related eczema. Babies most at risk are those born into families with a history of allergic disease and who have already shown allergic reactions to food such as eggs, and to a lesser extent cow's milk.

The risk seems to be greatest if the mother is atopic (see page 18). If you are, avoid eating peanuts during pregnancy and while breast-feeding. Other common allergens (the substance causing the allergy) such as tree nuts (peanuts are related to pulses and grow in the ground), sesame seed and eggs should also be avoided when breast-feeding. The symptoms of allergy appear within seconds or minutes of exposure. They include vomiting, itching, swelling of the lips, throat, tongue, face and head, difficulty in swallowing, hives or rashes anywhere on the body, flushing, abdominal cramp and asthma attack.

Degrees of reaction vary. In a severe generalised allergic reaction the body can go into life-threatening anaphylactic shock (see below), in which the swollen mouth and throat may cause suffocation. This does not happen on the first exposure, but may do with subsequent exposures.

It is unlikely that children will grow out of allergies, which are usually life-long, although a minority may develop tolerance and the severity of reaction may vary over time. There is no cure for allergy. The only way to avoid allergic reactions is to avoid the allergen.

Peanuts are not an essential part of an infant's diet. There are plenty of other protein foods – fish, poultry, lean meat, eggs, cheese, pulses such as lentils, split peas and beans – that can be given in appropriate consistencies at appropriate stages of weaning. After weaning, sub-stitutes for peanut butter such as hummus (a paste made from chickpeas, tahini – sesame seed spread – and oil) can be used. Although peanuts are a pulse and not a true nut, very few people with allergies to nuts have allergies to pulses (beans, soya, lentils, chickpeas and so on).

Sesame seed allergy

A growing number of people are also experiencing an allergy to sesame seed which can be potentially as serious as peanut allergy. It is estimated that about 1 in 2000 people suffers severe reactions to sesame seeds – although most are over the age of twenty-one. However, as the use of sesame seed is increasing for decoration and flavouring and in ethnic foods it is likely that babies will be exposed earlier and this allergy may increase to a similar level to peanut allergy.

What is food allergy?

Food allergy involves the immune system reacting inappropriately to food, or to an additive or ingredient in food. Food intolerance,

THE ABC OF HEALTHY EATING FOR BABIES AND TODDLERS

sometimes called false food allergy, can provoke the same symptoms but without involving the immune system.

An allergy to food causes the body to produce antibodies. Antibodies are proteins that neutralise antigens. Antigens are foreign proteins (for instance, viruses and bacteria) that trigger the production of antibodies. In a food allergy the food acts as an antigen to trigger a particular type of antibody attached to what are called mast cells. Once activated, the mast cells release powerful substances such as histamine and prostaglandins which cause the inflammation or sudden drop in blood pressure associated with an allergic reaction. In food intolerance the offending foods trigger mast cells to produce histamine, but antibodies are not involved.

The addresses listed on page 210 will provide further information.

Peanuts and cancer

Peanut butter has been periodically removed from sale in shops after batches have been found to contain high levels of aflatoxin, a mould that can cause cancer. Other nuts, such as brazils and pistachios, and dried figs are also particularly susceptible to aflatoxin, which can occur in cereals and many foods.

Food laws set limits for the amount of aflatoxin in foods, and if more than permitted levels are found manufacturers can be prosecuted. The latest surveys show that 88 per cent of peanut butter on sale contained less than the maximum amount allowed, but 12 per cent exceeded it; 97 per cent of dried figs contained less than the permitted amounts.

Peanuts for non-allergic infants

For children without allergies, nuts are a good source of protein, unsaturated fats and minerals. Even though peanuts are a common allergen smooth peanut butter is a popular weaning food, but introduction has always been delayed until eight months to a year as infants are most susceptible to developing food allergies in the first few months of life. Some experts are now suggesting that it might be sensible to delay introducing peanuts until the age of five or seven years for 'at risk' babies and children. However, doctors do not know if there is an age after which problems are less likely, and peanut allergies can develop at any age.

If toddlers are currently enjoying peanut butter without any adverse reaction, there is no need to stop eating peanut products in moderation as part of a balanced diet. There is no evidence to suggest that stopping eating them and reintroducing them after months or years will provoke the onset of an allergy.

FIRST AID FOR ANAPHYLACTIC SHOCK

Call an ambulance. Until help arrives, support the person in the position that most helps their breathing. Loosen their clothing at the neck and waist. If the person loses consciousness put them in the recovery position and be prepared to resuscitate. Severe allergy sufferers may carry adrenaline which is injected under the skin or into the muscle as soon as a severe reaction is suspected. They must go to hospital immediately.

PARENT ACTION

1. Delay the introduction of peanuts, or be especially vigilant when introducing them. Use only a small smear of peanut butter, for example. Be vigilant when introducing any other new foods, especially common allergens such as eggs, wheat and oranges. If your child is allergic to peanuts be careful with other nuts, pulses and seeds.

2. If you suspect that a child has a peanut allergy, consult your family doctor immediately. Allergic reactions are unpredictable and may vary in severity from one time to the next. Ask your GP for blood or skin tests or referral to a specialist, who will advise whether it is necessary to carry adrenaline in case of anaphylactic shock (see page 171). Adrenaline is available in an 'Epipen' format which automatically injects, with no need for needles and ampoules. The medication will have to be carried at all times.

3. If a nut or other allergy is confirmed, be scrupulous in avoiding foods that contain peanuts. If multiple allergies, or allergies to staple foods, are involved you will need help from a dietitian so that your child does not become malnourished. Speak to your family doctor about this, or contact the British Dietetic Association, the professional association for dietitians (for address see page 210).

4. If a nut allergy is confirmed, check for ingredients. Packaged foods have to be labelled with an ingredient list. Look out for peanuts on the labels of biscuits, breakfast cereal (e.g. nut corn flakes and muesli), confectionery (e.g. nougat) and chocolate bars, cakes, gateaux, savoury snacks, satay sauce and stuffing. There will be other foods, too, that contain nuts.

Foods sold loose do not need to list their ingredients, and of course restaurants and fast food outlets do not display lists of ingredients. Oriental cuisines such as Malay, Thai, Indonesian and Indian often use peanuts and peanut oil for cooking, as do takeaways. Shop assistants and waiters may not have accurate information about ingredients and garnishes. Contamination may occur in the kitchen unwittingly.

5. Even some artificial baby milks contain peanut oil. The ingredients list may just state 'vegetable oil', so check with the manufacturer, although most have removed it.

6. Peanuts can also appear on labels under other names such as groundnut, monkey nut and goober. Peanut oil may also be called arachis oil (from the botanical name of the peanut plant, *Arachis hypogaea*), groundnut oil, earthnut oil or monkey nut oil. It may be used for salad dressings, for packing canned sardines, and in the manufacture of mayonnaise, margarine and other cooking fats.

Blended 'vegetable oil' that does not specify the source may also contain it, and arachis oil is used in pharmaceuticals.

7. To avoid aflatoxin buy nuts and nut butters from shops with a speedy turnover of stock and use well within best before dates. In general, throw away any food that has mould on it, and certainly do not feed it to babies. It is not enough to cut off the mould, because invisible spores may have already penetrated deep into the rest of the food.

Phthalates in formula

Scary headlines about 'sex-change' or 'gender-bending' chemicals in baby milk inevitably frightened parents in May 1996. In the face of food scares such as peanuts or BSE you have a choice when shopping, but parents of bottle-fed babies cannot choose whether or not to give their babies formula. Formula is their babies' only food, and yet the future health of their children is at stake. The headlines related to the Ministry of Agriculture's release in March 1996 of the results of its monitoring of substances called phthalates in food. Fifteen brands of infant formula had been tested and all were found to contain low levels of phthalates, although some brands contained eight times more than others.

Some phthalates mimic the female hormone oestrogen, so scientists have linked them to falling human sperm counts, female infertility and breast cancer and think they might impair sexual development. Environmentalists link phthalates to feminisation of male gulls, fish and other wildlife.

The highest concentration found in the Ministry's monitoring programme was 10.2mg/kg, which would give a newborn 0.13 milligrams of phthalates for every kilogram of body weight per day, falling to 1.10mg/kg at six months. The upper level is above the lowest level at which one of the phthalates in the milk was found to damage the testicles of baby rats in experiments carried out by the Medical Research Council. But results are not strictly comparable, as testis development takes place over a longer time in humans than in rats.

While parents believe they have a right to know the facts so that they can choose the baby milk they feel safest, neither the Ministry of Agriculture (MAFF) nor the Department of Health (DoH) would name brands, insisting that there is no risk and going along with manufacturers of artificial baby milk who call the information 'commercially sensitive'. The government (backed by the EU, which demanded that the government provide details in order to protect consumers in Europe) maintains that the levels in baby milk are below Tolerable Daily Intakes (TDIs), amounts which are supposed not to cause harm over a normal lifetime's intake. However, the TDIs were set before recent findings that some phthalates behave like oestrogen. The same survey revealed phthalates in poultry, meat, eggs and milk – phthalates are stored in body fat.

Baby milk companies such as Cow & Gate, Milupa, SMA Nutrition and Farley's, which produce all fifteen brands on the market (all of which were affected), were asked to identify the source of contamination and reduce levels. Phthalates usually enter food during manufacture or packaging – they are plasticisers, materials used to soften plastics, especially PVC.

Six months after approaching the baby milk companies MAFF asked the manufacturers to speed up the search for the source of phthalates and thus the reduction of levels in formula. In that time the baby milk companies had ruled out the use of plasticisers as a source. MAFF set no deadline, neither did it impose any penalties or threat of penalties.

PARENT ACTION

1. Breastfeed rather than bottle-feed.
2. Keep yourself well informed on this issue (see consumer groups list and MAFF Consumer Helpline, both page 211).
3. Contact Baby Milk Action (for address see page 208), an independent non-profit organisation which raises awareness of the danger of artificial infant feeding and campaigns to protect infant health.
4. Write to your Member of Parliament at the House of Commons, London SW1A 0AA, or at the local constituency address, to ask for

full details of the findings – that is, exactly what was found in each brand. Ask also for research to be carried out into the effects of phthalates and their levels in commercial baby food and breastmilk. Ask for pressure to be put on baby milk companies to be open about their findings and identify the sources of contamination.

5. Write to your MP to ask for a ban on the use of PVC – Sweden, Denmark and parts of Germany have banned its use, although it is so widespread in the human food chain that removing it – and phthalates – from the environment altogether may prove impossible.

Hormones in soya formula

Scary headlines about artificial baby milk causing sex changes followed the discovery of quantities of naturally occurring plant hormones called phytoestrogens in soya-based infant formulas. In certain situations they can behave like a very weak form of the female hormone oestrogen. In animals this has caused some fertility problems, but little is known about the effect on human babies, whether unborn, newborn or as infants and young children.

In Japan and China, where large quantities of soya are eaten, there is no evidence of impaired fertility or altered sexual development, although regularly eating soya protein does affect women's menstrual cycle. On the plus side, soya is known to give some protection against certain types of cancer in adults. But as babies who are fed soya formula take in six times the amount of phytoestrogens known to have an effect on post-menopausal women, it is important to find out how these substances might affect infants.

Since 1992 the Committee on Toxicity of Chemicals in Food, Consumer Products and the Environment (COT), an independent committee that advises the government, has recommended further research to give a better understanding of the actions of phytoestrogens in the human body.

Levels of oestrogen in formula, cow's and breastmilk are set to be analysed, along with 300 samples of common plant foods. From this, MAFF will assess the likely intakes of infants and toddlers.

Although paediatricians are not finding large numbers of male infants exhibiting female sexual characteristics, the government has still asked food manufacturers to find ways of reducing phytoestrogen levels in their products.

The effects of phytoestrogens on a baby's cells will then be looked at, along with effects on pre-menopausal women and bones metabolism in men. From all these results MAFF plans to work out standards for acceptable levels of phytoestrogens in food.

Such sophisticated research will take months or even years. Meanwhile, the Department of Health assures parents that the oestrogen effect is too weak to cause sex changes or impair sex development in babies. Only 1 per cent of bottle-fed babies in the UK are fed soya formula.

PARENT ACTION

1. Until further research is available, the advice for parents from the Department of Health is continue to give your baby soya-based formula if you have been advised to do so on medical grounds.

2. If you have not been so advised, but have chosen soya-based formula because you are opposed to animal products or are vegan or for some other reason, continue with it, but seek advice from your doctor or health visitor.

3. Better still, breastfeed.

4. Write to your Member of Parliament at the House of Commons, London SW1A OAA, or at the local constituency address, to ask for full details of the findings and asking what research is to be carried out into the effects of phytoestrogens and when that research will be published.

5. If your baby is more than a year old you could introduce cow's milk, so long as no allergy or other reaction is suspected. Alternatively you could swap from formula to regular soya milk, as long as your child's nutritional requirements are being met by the rest of his or her diet. This may only be a problem in vegan families, in which it is sometimes the practice to give children soya formula until the age of five. Discuss with your doctor or health visitor.

Dioxins in breastmilk

These highly toxic and persistent chemicals are produced in the manufacture of chemicals, including chlorine, and by the incineration of PVC and other materials. They are released into the air, fall on plants and are eaten by animals, where they become concentrated in their body fat. The main source of dioxins for humans is food. Dioxins can pass through the placenta to the fetus and into breastmilk, which contains relatively high levels of dioxins, although levels in breastmilk fell by about 35 per cent between 1988 and 1994.

The estimated intake of breastfed babies from first-time mothers in the UK is currently 110pg (picograms) per kilogram of body weight per day for a two-month-old baby, falling to 26pg at ten months. Dioxins in the breastmilk of mothers feeding their second or subsequent child are generally lower. A Tolerable Daily Intake (TDI) of 10pg per kilogram of body weight per day has been set by the COT. This means that babies are getting around ten times more than the TDI. However, the COT does not consider that breastfeeding greatly increases total dioxin intake over a lifetime. It considers that the benefits of breastfeeding outweigh any potential harmful side-effects such as effect on fertility.

Dioxins (and other chemicals such as PCBs or polychlorinated biphenyls) also have close structural similarities to thyroid hormones, which are essential for fetal development. By mimicking the action of key hormones they may be responsible for reduced IQ and learning disorders. Scientists think that there may be no safe level of exposure to these endocrine-disrupting chemicals, because they are so widespread in the environment and persistent that they can pass from generation to generation.

PARENT ACTION

1. Do not be put off breastfeeding because of the presence of dioxins in human milk.

2. Avoidance of dioxins would seem to be impossible as they are a general environmental pollutant. If you want to protest about the

THE ABC OF HEALTHY EATING FOR BABIES AND TODDLERS

situation, contact your MP at the House of Commons, London SW1A OAA, to demand more research and publicity into the effects of dioxins and more action to limit exposure to them. For example, tighter controls on the use of PVC (some EU countries have recently decided to stop the use of PVC, which, incidentally, is also one of the biggest sources of phthalates: see page 174). You could also join an environmental lobbying group such as Greenpeace or Friends of the Earth, or an organisation promoting organic agriculture which does not use harmful chemicals, such as the Soil Association. Or you could join the National Childbirth Trust, which also lobbies for more information on chemicals and other substances that are a potential cause of harm to fertility and babies. (To contact any of these organisations, see Useful Addresses page 207.)

The risk from artificial sweeteners

One in 18 children and one in 12 toddlers (aged from one and a half to two and a half years) is exceeding the safe saccharin intake. High-level consumers in this age group are ingesting 6.4 milligrams per kilogram of body weight per day, slightly more than the ADI (Acceptable Daily Intake, the amount considered safe over a lifetime's normal consumption) of 5mg per kilogram of body weight per day set by the COT.

The COT does not consider occasionally exceeding the ADI to have any adverse effects on the health of the children concerned. It is

felt extremely unlikely that any of the children currently exceeding the ADI will continue to do so as their diet will change over time. However, there is no evidence that children who habitually consume soft drinks, fizzy drinks and other highly sweetened foods will change their habits. All research to date suggests it is very difficult to get people to change to healthier eating habits.

Despite the COT's lack of concern, the committee recommended that for children under the age of four more water should be added to concentrated soft drinks (a major source of artificial sweeteners) than for adults. The COT also wants to see appropriate dilution advice printed on the labels of soft drinks, in leaflets and available through clinics for young children. Recent changes in EU regulations covering soft drinks mean that parents need to be even more vigilant about the widespread use of artificial sweeteners. Previous regulations requiring only sugar to be added to soft drinks have been dropped, and an increasing number of regular (not diet or reduced sugar) soft drinks are being sweetened with artificial sweeteners, which are cheaper than sugar. Under EU labelling regulations, drinks that contain sweeteners have to state 'with sweetener' in the full name of the drink – but only tucked away in the small print – not on the front of the bottle, as some campaigners had hoped.

Typical intake of soft drinks among toddlers is 350–340ml a day, equivalent to one can. A carton contains around 250ml. According to the Food Commission, a single carton of ready-to-drink soft drink sweetened with cyclamates, two cartons sweetened with acesulfame K, or three to four cartons sweetened with aspartame or saccharine could be excessive for a typical toddler. In other words, any of these could take a toddler over the ADI.

Even less could put toddlers over the top if their drinks contain more than the permitted maximum level of 80mg of saccharin per litre. Recent analyses by local authority trading standards officers have shown that it is not unusual for drinks to contain too much saccharin – which may be only one of several sweeteners used in each product.

However, soft drinks are not the only source of sweeteners of which parents need to be aware. Sweeteners are also commonly used in yogurt, savoury snacks, instant desserts, jelly, custard, ice lollies,

THE ABC OF HEALTHY EATING FOR BABIES AND TODDLERS

rice pudding, baked beans and even toothpaste. Use of sweeteners is rarely declared on the front of packs.

PARENT ACTION

1. It may be harder work, but there are other ways to pacify fractious tots than to give them a sugary drink. Do not give them squash or other concentrates. Do not give them fizzy drinks. Instead offer diluted unsweetened fruit juice at mealtimes, or very diluted between meals if necessary. Otherwise stick to water and milk.

2. Read labels carefully. The new EU directive with which manufacturers have to comply by July 1997 requires them to state alongside the name of the drink whether it contains sugar, sweeteners or both – for example, Joe Blogg's Soft Drink with sugar and/or artificial sweetener. But while dentists and other health professionals wanted the precise type of sweetener to be stated on the front of the label, the industry has managed to lobby so that the complete name can be tucked away in small print elsewhere on the label.

3. Follow dilution instructions carefully. The same EU directive rules that soft drinks have to replace 'dilute to taste' with 'dilute X parts of cordial with X parts of water'. This is mainly to prevent consumption of too much preservative, but should also help stop your child taking in too much artificial sweetener.

Patulin in apple juice

After high levels of the mycotoxin patulin (a poisonous mould) were found in apple juice, an advisory level of 50 micrograms per kilogram was set in 1992. Advisory levels are not legally binding. However, since 1992 MAFF has surveyed apple juice annually to check whether manufacturers are complying. The trend has been for the majority of samples tested to be below 50mcg/kg. However, in 1995 a substantial 6 per cent of samples contained amounts of patulin at or well above the level. The government has again asked – but not insisted – that the food industry sticks to the guidelines.

1. Since the government has failed to set and enforce mandatory levels, the best advice is to avoid directly produced apple juice (juice not made from concentrate), which is most likely to contain high levels of patulin. Stick to juice made from concentrate and dilute it well.

2. If you buy from a small producer/farm, ask if they check their apples for patulin. Many small producers do not undertake routine analysis for mould before juicing fruit. MAFF is researching a cheap and simple test for use on the farm. It has also advised juice producers to use only high-quality fruit stored at low temperature in controlled (low oxygen) conditions. The fruit should not be kept at room temperature for long before juicing.

Herbal drinks for babies and toddlers

Herbal baby drinks continue to increase in popularity. Experts such as those responsible for the COMA report on weaning have questioned the need for such drinks. They advise that herbal drinks for babies should not contain herbal constituents which are not part of the normal diet; neither should the herbs in them be given at concentrations higher than normally found in food. Concern centres on the possible harmful side-effects of the natural constituents of herbs. COMA has asked the Department of Health for more advice on the safety of herbal ingredients. Parents will also be concerned about the other ingredients (for instance sugar, maltodextrin and skimmed milk powder) in these drinks, which are often dried powders reconstituted with water. They may be harmful to teeth because of their sugar content and acidity.

PARENT ACTION

1. Once again there seems to be a lack of effective protection for babies and young children. As the experts say, there is no reason for babies and toddlers to have these drinks. In my view these drinks are just produced to enhance manufacturers' profits by

creating a new niche market for baby products. The manufacturers are, I think, taking advantage of parents' perception that there might be natural benefits in herbs and that these are inherently safe and natural products. They are also cashing in on parents' search for alternatives to sugary drinks or on their concerns about sweeteners. I would stick to milk, water or well-diluted unsweetened fruit juice as appropriate.

2. Herbs can be very beneficial in the treatment of common conditions. For example, both camomile and fennel are used in herbal teas for babies with colic; while thyme is used for coughs, colds and ear, nose and throat infections in children. But peppermint tea should not be given to children under four. The best way to use herbs is with the advice of a qualified medical herbalist. For your nearest practitioner contact the National Institute of Medical Herbalists (see Useful Addresses page 205).

Keep yourself up-to-date on food issues

Subscribe to organisations that keep abreast of the issues relating to your baby or toddler's diet and health, and respond on behalf of the consumer. Consider the Food Commission's publication *The Food Magazine*, the National Childbirth Trust's magazine *New Generation*, and *Health Which?*, published by the Consumers' Association (see Useful Addresses page 211).

Honey ban for babies

Fears about babies getting botulism (a very serious form of food poisoning) from eating honey have led the Department of Health and British honey importers and packers to recommend that honey should not be given to babies under twelve months. There have been no cases in the UK (yet), but in the US 'floppy baby syndrome' has resulted after babies have eaten bacterial spores (*Clostridium*

botulinum) in honey. The symptoms include lethargy and constipation, but it can be far more serious than that.

Cases of botulism usually result after the toxins that have been produced by the organism are eaten in food (heat, and therefore cooking, does not destroy these toxins): for example, in outbreaks associated with canned salmon or sausages or pâté. But in infantile botulism it is the actual spores that cause problems for babies whose immature digestive tract can become colonised by the spores, which produce the toxin in their guts.

PARENT ACTION

1. 'Is there honey still for tea . . .?' Follow the experts' advice and do not feed honey to babies under a year old.

Bottle-feeding and diabetes

Giving 'at risk' babies formula or cow's milk too early in life has been blamed for the recent doubling in the number of under-fives developing insulin-dependent diabetes (IDDM). Despite the headlines that suggest this as fact, it is still only a theory.

The causes of IDDM are not known. What we do know is this:

- Babies who were not breastfed or were breastfed for only a short time are at increased (1.5-fold) risk of diabetes
- Babies who were exposed to cow's milk in the first few months of life are at increased (1.5-fold) risk of diabetes
- Up to 100 per cent of newly diagnosed diabetic patients have antibodies to bovine serum albumen (a protein in cow's milk)
- In experiments on animals, feeding with cow's milk increases the number that develop diabetes

However, evidence from some studies conflicts with these findings, which do not prove that formula made from modified cow's milk is the trigger for diabetes in babies who are genetically predisposed to the disease. Neither do the findings so far mean that you will prevent your baby developing diabetes if their diet is free from cow's milk.

1. This one is a case of wait-and-see what more research brings forth . . .

2. For more information contact the British Diabetic Association (see Useful Addresses page 206).

Hyperactivity and diet

ADHA (Attention Deficit Hyperactivity Disorder), to use the latest name, has consistently been linked to diet – although one view is that it is a convenient excuse for ineffectual parenting that results in unruly behaviour. According to the Hyperactive Children's Support Group (which has worked tirelessly for nearly twenty years to identify the causes and help parents work out strategies for coping), 50 per cent of hyperactive children respond to a diet free from synthetic additives and natural salicylates. Others respond to a milk-free and wheat-free diet.

Salicylates, to which these children may be sensitive, are found in some fruits and vegetables such as apricots, grapes, raisins and tomatoes. They are chemically similar to aspirin. Some recent findings suggest that hyperactivity is linked to a deficiency of essential fatty acids.

Hyperactivity is thought to have a genetic origin. Many hyperactive children are atopic and also suffer from repeated chest and ear infections, and they are often constantly thirsty. The condition is most common among blue-eyed blond boys.

PARENT ACTION

1. Before trying to exclude any major foods from your child's diet consult your doctor, health visitor or other health professional.

2. For more information contact the Hyperactive Children's Support Group for their guide *Hyperactive Children: a guide to their management* (see Useful Addresses page 212).

Squash can stunt children's growth

So said the headlines about 'Squash Drinking Syndrome', in which too much fruit squash and fruit juice was linked to sickly, malnourished children. The syndrome was identified by researchers at the University of Southampton in 1995, who found some children derived between 30 and 50 per cent of their calories from fruit squash. Not surprisingly, the children were not gaining weight properly and had poor appetite, irritability and diarrhoea. A serving of blackcurrant squash contains the equivalent of three teaspoons of sugar per 100ml after dilution. An average beaker therefore contains six to nine teaspoons of sugar – empty calories without any vitamins and minerals for growing toddlers. Swapping the squash and fruit juice for milk would improve the children's health and weight gain. But better still, their calories should come from a well-balanced diet – and less drink.

PARENT ACTION

1. Start as you mean to go on. Try to resist pressure from advertising, friends and family to give your baby sweet drinks from an early age. Milk or water are preferable, both at meals and between meals, if needed. Yet surveys suggest that around 70 per cent of pre-school children never drink plain water. While a limited amount of fruit juice may be beneficial and a good source of vitamin C, giving children a lot is not a healthy option because drinks do not contain other vitamins, starchy carbohydrates, fat, minerals or protein to build bones and muscles.

BSE ('Mad Cow' disease)

Many parents must have been left in a state of confusion in March 1996 when the chairman of the independent expert advisory committee on BSE and CJD (Creutzfeldt-Jakob disease, the human equivalent of mad cow disease) said he would not feed beef to his three-month-old grandson who had never

eaten meat, but that he would continue to give it to his nine-month-old granddaughter! After addressing the question, 'Is beef safe for our children to eat?', the committee concluded that 'if human infection with the BSE agent occurs, infants and children are not likely to be more susceptible to that infection than are adults'. Pregnant women and other 'at risk' groups were also told that none of them was likely to have any increased susceptibility to the infection.

Since then, the probable cause of the increase in cases of a new type of CJD has been attributed to eating the agent that causes BSE in cattle. And while the government assures us that current controls will prevent that BSE agent getting into our food, prosecutions continue because food manufacturers are not complying with the regulations.

Meanwhile scientists are still trying to find out the exact nature of the agent that causes the new variant of CJD, and to work out the link between BSE and CJD and whether BSE can pass to humans as the new type of CJD. They are also trying to develop new diagnostic tests for early detection of the disease before diseased animals get into the human food chain.

The truth is that no one knows if eating infected beef causes CJD in humans, although by the government's own admission the rise in cases of a new strain of CJD among young people is most likely to have been caused by consuming BSE. No one knows whether it takes just one bite of infected meat to pass on BSE, or whether (as seems more likely) it is related to the amount eaten. No one really knows whether infants are more susceptible than other age groups. If they are more susceptible to all other diseases it is not logical to think that they will be less susceptible to CJD – although, as with AIDS, because it is incurable they are probably at the same risk as adults.

No one really knows how BSE is passed on, but it can be passed from cow to calf and it can be transmitted to other species – most recently sheep. No one knows if BSE can be passed on via milk, although it is thought unlikely.

WHAT IS BSE?

BSE, or bovine spongiform encephalopathy, turns the brains of infected cattle spongy (hence the name). The cattle tremble, stagger and suffer uncontrollable muscle spasms before dying. The disease may be caused by a prion, a protein without DNA that replicates itself uncontrollably and cannot be broken down by the body. More than half of British dairy herds and 15 per cent of beef suckler herds have had one or more cases of BSE. The fear, of course, is that the disease might be transmitted to humans who would suffer it in the form of CJD.

WHAT IS CJD?

CJD is a rare degenerative brain disease that is fatal and does not show symptoms until years after the original infection. The disease causes muscular contractions and dementia with loss of speech; the person becomes vegetative and their body goes rigid.

A long-term study of deaths from CJD is being carried out to identify any changes in the pattern since the emergence of BSE. The incidence of CJD rose in the UK in 1994, from 42 cases in the previous year to 55. It remains at a similar rate to other countries worldwide, including those without BSE. However, the incidence of teenagers suffering CJD is very rare, and the chance of four dairy farmers getting this disease by coincidence has been calculated at 10,000 to one.

WHEN DID BSE START, AND WHAT HAS BEEN DONE TO STOP IT?

An epidemic of BSE in cattle was recognised in the mid-1980s. It became a notifiable disease in 1988, after which all affected cattle were ordered to be slaughtered and incinerated. In addition, in 1989 specified bovine offals were ordered to be removed from cattle over six months of age at the slaughterhouse, dyed to distinguish them, and then destroyed.

THE ABC OF HEALTHY EATING FOR BABIES AND TODDLERS

According to the Ministry of Agriculture (MAFF) even cattle fed large amounts of infective agent have not shown infectivity under eighteen months of age. The ban on the use of specified bovine offals is intended to ensure that if any cattle are in the early stages of the disease, when symptoms are not apparent, the offals, in which the organism that causes BSE in infected cattle are concentrated, do not enter the food chain. The specified offals are brain, spinal cord, tonsil, intestine, thymus and spleen.

Crushed bones, fat, gristle, sinew, skin and any other material from cattle that is not listed as specified offals can be used in what is called mechanically recovered meat (MRM). Mechanically recovered bovine meat is not listed as an ingredient in foods, but will merely appear on food ingredients lists as 'beef'.

In December 1995, in a move to tighten up BSE controls, the government banned the use of bovine vertebral column in MRM as 'a precautionary measure to remove the risk of spinal cord tissue entering the human food chain', and to protect us from any 'remote theoretical risk of BSE'. Although spinal columns should have been removed and destroyed since 1989, checks by vets at slaughterhouses revealed that small amounts of spinal cord were being left in some carcasses used for the manufacture of MRM. Other procedures were not being carried out correctly.

In 1996 carcasses from cattle aged over thirty months started to be deboned in specially licensed and supervised plants and trimmings from these animals were kept out of the food chain. Also, meat and bonemeal from any mammals were banned from feed for any farm animals, to prevent the possible spread of BSE to pigs or chickens. There is now concern that BSE has spread to chickens.

WHAT CAUSED BSE?

One theory about the cause of the BSE epidemic is that lower temperatures introduced in the 1980s for rendering down sheep offal for use in animal feedstuffs no longer destroyed the agent that caused scrapie (a similar brain disease) in sheep. The agent then passed to cattle, in which it caused BSE, either in its original form or

in a new one. Scrapie has been present in sheep in Britain for at least 250 years without evidence of causing human health problems.

IS ORGANIC BEEF SAFER?

There seem to be fewer incidents of BSE in cattle on organic farms. This may be because the majority have not been given contaminated feed, or because they have not been treated with organophosphates or OPs, (pesticides that are known neurotoxins). Some authorities think OPs have made cattle susceptible to the agent that caused the BSE epidemic, and even people susceptible to the new variants of CJD.

IS MILK SAFE?

BSE has never been found in milk which has been tested for it.

WILL COOKING DESTROY BSE?

If the infective agent for BSE was found in red meat or other meat products, domestic cooking would not destroy it. Temperatures high enough to destroy the agent would make the meat inedible.

WHERE ELSE IS BEEF IN OUR FOOD?

Beef and beef products might be found in any unspecified 'meat' (pies, sausages, pâté and so on), stocks, meat extracts, gravy granules and soups, also as gelatine in yogurts and other dairy desserts, confectionery and jelly.

PARENT ACTION

1. All of this uncertainty leaves parents, in my view, with only one option. Avoid all beef products for infants (and yourselves) until we know the answers. Use other meats, or vegetable alternatives, as appropriate.

THE ABC OF HEALTHY EATING FOR BABIES AND TODDLERS

Pesticides

More than three hundred pesticides are available to farmers and growers in the UK. They are tested on animals for toxicity, and from the effects Acceptable Daily Intakes (ADIs: see box page 195) are worked out. Although government experts assure us that ADIs take into account infants and young children, some lobbyists say that wider safety margins are needed to protect the young.

Weight for weight, children eat much more fruit, vegetables, fruit juices, milk and other foods that commonly contain pesticide residues than adults do. They consume more than double the calories of food per unit of body weight than adults do. Children's metabolic rate is twice that of adults, yet because of differences in body composition (such as ratio of water to fat and protein) they retain toxins for longer than adults, and have a lower capacity to excrete pollutants such as pesticide residues. Their immature organs and body systems are more susceptible to damage from potential carcinogens – which some pesticides are – and other harmful chemicals such as lead. Babies and children have a rapid rate of growth with significant brain development up to the age of six. In the first year of life 55–60 per cent of energy (calories) consumed is for brain development.

Taking these and other factors into consideration, it has been estimated that the toxic effect of pesticides may be between five and ten times greater in children than in adults. Some researchers suggest that sensitivity in children may be up to 150 times that of adults.

However, very little data exists on the specific effects of pesticides on the young – most toxicity tests have been done on adult animals. This makes it impossible to answer the questions that most parents raise: How toxic are pesticides to my baby or toddler? What is the exact level of exposure during weaning and early childhood? What might the side-effects of typical exposure be?

Babies and children cannot assess the risks for themselves or take action to avoid any food that may be harming them, so it is up to parents. The British Medical Association (the UK doctors' professional organisation) recognises that babies and children are especially vulnerable to pesticide residues and has called for a review of pesticide policy.

Children's intake of pesticide residue foods

Weight for weight, children drink seventeen times more apple juice than adults, three times as much orange juice and eight times as much milk. They eat seven times more apples, twice as many pears and carrots and twice as much chicken, beef and flour. This means that babies and toddlers may already exceed the acceptable intake for adults of pesticides in many foods, especially the relatively unprocessed foods such as fresh fruit and vegetables and meat that parents are encouraged to use during weaning.

However, it is impossible to make an exact assessment of the pesticide levels in our food because only one food item is tested for residues per 100 million food items bought by UK shoppers. Of those tested for pesticides, more than one in every hundred contains levels above the Maximum Residue Level (MRL, defined on page 195), and 30 per cent of those contain pesticide residues at so-called Acceptable Daily Intake levels.

Some American environmentalists estimate that by the age of five most children will have already taken in as many pesticide residues as they should in a lifetime.

THE ENVIRONMENTAL BENEFITS OF ORGANIC FOOD

Organic food not only protects a child's health but, through the system of sustainable agriculture which produces it, aims to protect the environment for your child's future.

Organic food is often criticised for being expensive. That is because it does not benefit from the subsidies given to producers of the so-called cheap food which we find in the supermarket, which is seen as a miracle of modern chemical-dependent agriculture. Some

THE ABC OF HEALTHY EATING FOR BABIES AND TODDLERS

might say that pesticides are the unacceptable face of this 'cheap' food.

In fact, are we really enjoying cheap food? Not if you take into account:

- The £1billion a year cost of removing pesticides from the water supply
- The £1.4billion slaughter bill to combat BSE
- Massive EU subsidies (under the heavily criticised Common Agricultural Policy) for current abuses of animal welfare
- The cost of acid rain
- Greenhouse gas emission
- The loss of wildlife and destruction of the countryside
- The exploitation of Third World countries to produce cheap food for the West

Add these on to the low prices achieved through supermarket price wars and you will see that what we pay at the checkout is not a true reflection of the cost of food.

In addition, intensive farming systems can result in reduced nutritional quality of food. New plant varieties grown in Asia's Green Revolution (see page 108) are so nutritionally deficient that a loss of 10 IQ points had been seen in a generation of children reared on crops grown this way. It is not known if children in the West are similarly affected.

Can you wash off pesticides?

Washing fresh fruit and vegetables will remove surface pesticide residues, but most pesticides are 'systemic'. That is they are taken into the vegetable or fruit as it grows, becoming part of its content. Residues are also likely to be higher in fresher produce as the pesticide may diminish over time. Fruit should be peeled for babies and toddlers.

PESTICIDES IN BABY FOOD

The testing of baby foods for pesticide residues is inadequate. They are tested only on a three-year cycle: one year meat-based foods are tested, the next fruit and the next cereal. The tests are carried out by the government's Working Party on Pesticide Residues. The latest survey of pesticides in baby foods analysed sixty samples of dehydrated infant food for residues of inorganic bromide and other pesticides. The samples were 25 per cent infant breakfast (mostly cereal-based), 50 per cent infant dinners (mostly vegetable- and meat-based) and 25 per cent infant desserts (mostly fruit- and milk-based). Inorganic bromide was the only residue found at or above the limit at which it has to be reported – 3 milligrams per kilogram – in 10 per cent of the samples. According to MAFF, it may have been present from natural sources.

Seventy meat-based infant foods were also analysed and residues were found in 10 per cent of samples: DDT in one, dieldrin in one, endosulfan in two and gamma-HCH in three. There are no MRLs (see page 195) for these pesticides as they are banned and should not therefore be present.

No multiple residues were found in the samples tested.

To put the baby food findings in context, the 1995 report revealed pesticide residues in 31 per cent of the samples tested; MRLs were exceeded in 1 per cent of samples. In other words, at least one third of all non-organic baby foods that you might buy are likely to contain pesticide residues.

THE ABC OF HEALTHY EATING FOR BABIES AND TODDLERS

How Acceptable Daily Intakes for pesticides are set

Pesticides are tested to establish an Acceptable Daily Intake (ADI), the amount of the chemical which, according to the government's Advisory Committee on Pesticides, can be consumed every day for the average individual's whole lifetime without harm. The ADI is measured in milligrams per kilogram of body weight. It includes a 100 times safety margin, less the NEL (the No Effect Level, the highest dose at which no adverse effects appear when tested on adult animals). This margin assumes that a human is ten times more sensitive than the most sensitive animal and that the most sensitive man is ten times more sensitive than the average. It also assumes that humans are affected in exactly the same way as animals – which they are not.

The ADI provides the basis for the Maximum Residue Level (MRL), which is really a guide to good pesticide use for growers. The MRL is set at the maximum residue of a pesticide in milligrams per kilogram which should result when the correct dose of pesticide is applied at the correct rate by the grower. The MRL is set below the likely level of that pesticide which might be ingested from all food sources.

Using the results of animal testing as guidelines for the safety of pesticides where humans are concerned is not ideal, and in America the US National Research Council (NRC) has concluded that current permissible levels of pesticides in food do not adequately protect infants and children. The rapid growth of babies, their faster metabolism, their sensitivity at critical stages of development, and their immature endocrine, immune and reproductive systems make them particularly vulnerable to toxins such as pesticide residues. The UK government's Pesticides Safety Directorate has been informed of the NRC report and says that ADIs do take into account vulnerable groups of consumers such as infants. This is a matter of controversy.

LINDANE IN COW'S MILK AND FORMULA

Parents are encouraged to wean babies on to cow's milk and dairy products and to make milk and its products a staple food for infants. So it is disturbing to discover from MAFF surveys undertaken in 1995 that one pint of milk in every 24 in the UK contained amounts of the pesticide lindane above the MRL. Ninety-nine samples out of 216 were contaminated. And if this pesticide residue is in milk it will also be present in formula (see also the discussion of phthalates on page 174 and soya on page 176). Some cheese made at the same time also exceeded the MRL for lindane. Following an investigation the government said that the lindane levels found in milk did not pose a health risk, even to babies. By the beginning of 1996 these residues had returned to 'normal background levels'. The same survey also found DDT residues in two samples, even though DDT has been banned in Britain for more than ten years.

Lindane is an organochlorine insecticide used on crops such as rape, sugar beet, wheat and root crops. It has been linked to health problems including breast cancer (twice the national rate occurs in sugar beet-growing areas) and blood disorders and is banned in fourteen countries, but continues to be used in Britain.

ORGANOPHOSPHOROUS RESIDUES IN CARROTS

Unexpectedly high levels (up to twenty-five times those in previous findings) of these potentially dangerous pesticide residues in carrots resulted in government advice to peel carrots and cut off the tops 'as an added precaution'. Yet according to some experts this will only remove some of the residues because many of the pesticides in use are systemic, which means they penetrate beyond the skin. Analyses of carrots have revealed that single carrots can contain residues of three different pesticides at more than ten times the ADI.

Government response to these findings are that carrots remain 'safe and nutritious and that consumers need have no concern about retaining them as staple items of their diet. Consumers generally need to increase their consumption of fruit and vegetables . . .'

Organophosphates are known to be particularly toxic: in military contexts they are used as nerve gas. Farmers suffer a variety of illnesses caused by former compulsory use of organophosphorous pesticides in sheep dip. Although pesticide poisoning among farmers might be due to a massive single dose or doses, the effect of organophosphates is also cumulative and as exposure increases damage becomes more severe. Children are particularly sensitive to exposure to chemicals at critical stages of their development.

Monitoring continues and, in the wake of government recommendations to limit to only three applications of organophosphates per carrot crop, there has been some reduction in pesticide residues.

PARENT ACTION

1. Buy organically produced meat, milk, fruit and vegetables, flour and so on. Organic agriculture does not use pesticides and other agrochemicals, making it a safer system for health and the environment. Several British symbols show that a food has been produced to organic standards, which do not allow the use of pesticides and other agrochemicals. The most widespread and best-established symbol is that of the Soil Association. For details contact the Organic Food and Farming Centre (see Useful Addresses page 211).

There are other approved systems of organic production registered with UKROFS (the UK Register of Organic Food Standards): the Irish Organic Farmers' and Growers' Association, the Organic Farmers and Growers, the Organic Food Federation, the Scottish Organic Producers' Association and the Biodynamic Agricultural Association's 'Demeter' sign.

See Chapter 3 for recommended brands of organically produced baby food.

2. Don't let pesticide panic stop you from giving your children lots of fruit and vegetables. The balance of evidence is that not eating enough of these foods is linked to some forms of cancer later in life, while there is no evidence to suggest that pesticide residues in food have caused cancer.

3. All fresh produce, whether organic or not, should be washed well before use. In addition peel all non-organic fruit for toddlers.

4. Demand more systematic and extensive surveillance of baby foods such as annual analyses of wet food in jars. Write to your MP or direct to MAFF.

5. Demand a reassessment of the current safety levels of pesticide residues in baby foods.

Nitrates in vegetables

Nitrates are a type of artificial fertiliser. High nitrate intakes have been linked to cancer. Routine sampling of vegetables in the UK shows that growers routinely exceed new limits proposed by the EU for nitrate residues in lettuce and spinach. The MAFF reaction has been to veto the proposals because British growers say it would not be economically viable for them to meet the new safer, lower levels. The government affirms that UK consumers are well within its own ADIs for nitrates when eating spinach and lettuce. However, despite this assurance, a national one-year monitoring programme for nitrates in spinach and lettuce has been set up by MAFF. Highest residue levels seem to occur between August and October.

In addition to concerns about winter lettuce and spinach, the most recent report of the government's Working Party on Pesticides Residues discloses other continued misuse of pesticides – despite supposed MAFF enforcement action. Nearly one-third of UK-grown pears also contain residues of pesticides not even approved for use in the UK. Celery, cress and watercress also habitually contain higher than desirable levels of pesticide residues.

PARENT ACTION

1. See Parent Action for pesticides, page 197.

Antimony in food and cot death

Following suggestions that high levels of the trace element antimony were linked to cot death (Sudden Infant Death Syndrome), a survey of fifty baby and infant foods and milks was undertaken by MAFF. Samples were analysed for eight trace elements, molybdenum, thallium, titanium and vanadium. Some of these are essential in minute amounts but harmful in excess. In all the foods tested concentrations were either very low or too low to detect, leading to the conclusion that exposure to these substances by the very young would be very low. However, one sample of infant food contained high levels of chromium. The findings were not repeated at further tests and it was attributed to contamination during manufacturing.

PARENT ACTION

1. No recommendation.

Salmonella in eggs and other food

It is nearly a decade since Edwina Currie lost her ministerial job after speaking out about the dangers of salmonella food poisoning from eggs. Although the government instigated tough new regulations on egg production (and subsequent improvements in food hygiene), it is still not safe for babies and other 'vulnerable' people such as pregnant women (see page 25) to eat raw eggs or uncooked foods made from them. Chicken and turkey also commonly contain salmonella. Any food poisoning in babies is dangerous because it can lead to rapid dehydration (through vomiting and diarrhoea) and shock.

WHY DID SALMONELLA BECOME SUCH A PROBLEM?

Very briefly, the increase in two particular types of salmonella – enteritidis and typhimurium – in poultry and in laying flocks has been attributed to factory farming conditions and to the feeding of infected chicken meat to other chickens.

PARENT ACTION

1. Babies and toddlers should only be given eggs which have been cooked until the white and yolk are solid. So soft boiled eggs, poached and fried eggs with runny yolks and scrambled eggs are off the menu.
2. Poultry and all meat for babies and toddlers needs to be carefully defrosted (where appropriate) and cooked thoroughly to destroy any salmonella and other food poisoning bacteria present.
3. Follow good hygiene practices (page 109) to avoid food salmonella poisoning.

A B C

Selected References

References listed in order of appearance in text.

The National Diet and Nutrition Survey: pre-school children aged 1½ to 4½ years, commissioned by the Ministry of Agriculture, Fisheries and Food (MAFF) and the Department of Health (DoH), undertaken by the Office of Population Census and Surveys and the Medical Research Council Dunn Nutrition Unit 1992–93, published HMSO, London, 1995
Vol. 2: *The National Child Dental Health Survey of the UK*

Professor David Barker of the Research Council's Environmental Epidemiology Unit, Southampton General Hospital – twenty-one papers showing the relationship between birth weight at the lower end of the normal range to health problems later in life. Two summaries: *The Fetal Origins of Adult Disease*, Wellcome Foundation Lecture, 1994, and 'The Unbearable Lightness at Birth', *Science and Public Affairs*, Royal Society, Spring 1996:33–7

'Growth in Utero and Cognitive Function in Adult Life: follow-up study of people born between 1920 and 1943', C. Martyn, C. Gale, A. Sayer, C. Fall, MRC Environmental Epidemiology Unit, University of Southampton, Southampton General Hospital, *British Medical Journal (BMJ)*, 1996, 312:1393–6

'Intelligence and the X Chromosome', Professor Gillian Turner, *Lancet*, 1996, 347:1814–15

'Maternal Nutrition in Early and Late Pregnancy in Relation to Placental and Fetal Growth', K. Godfrey, S. Robinson, D.P.J. Barker, C. Osmond, V. Cox, *BMJ*, 1996, 312:410–4

'Introducing the Infant's First Solid Food', Dr Gillian Harris, Birmingham University, 1993, *British Food Journal*, Vol. 95, no. 9:7–10

'Development of Taste Preferences: implications for nutrition and health', Z. Warwick, *Nutrition Today*, March/April 1990

'Eating Habits and Attitudes of Mothers of Children with Non-organic Failure to Thrive', J. McCann, A. Stein, C. Fairburn, D. Dunger *Archives of Diseases in Childhood*, 1994, 70:234–6

'Maternal Nutrition in Early and Late Pregnancy in Relation to Placental and Fetal Growth', K. Godfrey, S. Robinson, D.P.J. Barker, C. Osmond, V. Cox, *BMJ*, 1996, 312:410–14

'Cohort Study of Peanut and Tree Nut Sensitisation by Age of 4 Years', S.M. Tariq, M. Stevens, S. Matthews, S. Ridout, R. Twiselton, D.W. Hide, *BMJ*, 1996, 313:514–7

'Clinical Study of Peanut and Nut Allergy in 62 Consecutive Patients: new features and associations', P.M. Ewan, *BMJ* 1996, 312:1074–8

'Peanut Allergy in Relation to Heredity, Maternal Diet, and Other Atopic Diseases', J. O'B. Hourihane, T.P. Dean, J.O. Warner, *BMJ*, 1996, 313:518–21

'Managing Peanut Allergy', H. Sampson, director, Paediatric Clinical Research Centre, Johns Hopkins University School of Medicine, Baltimore, USA, *BMJ*, 1996 312:1050–1

'Maternal Obesity Increases Congenital Malformations', *Nutrition Reviews*, 54:146–52

'Is It Worthwhile Breast-feeding?', J.S. Forsyth, *European Journal of Clinical Nutrition*, 1992, Vol. 46, Supplement 1:19–25

'Breastfeeding – the Immunological Case', J. Brock, *New Generation Digest*, December 1993:5–6

'Vitamin K and Childhood Cancer: a population based case-control study in Lower Saxony, Germany', *BMJ*, 1996, 313:199–203

'Childhood Leukaemia and Intramuscular Vitamin K: findings from a case-control study', *BMJ*, 1996, 313:204–5

'Vitamin K at Birth', editorial, *BMJ* 1996, 313:179–8

Dietary Reference Values for Food Energy and Nutrients for the United Kingdom, report of the panel on Dietary Reference Values of the Committee on Medical Aspects of Food Policy, HMSO, 1991

'Herbal Products and Breastfeeding', P. Golightly, *New Generation Digest*, June 1996

'Effect of Diet on the Fatty Acid Composition of the Major Phospholips of Infant Cerebral Cortex', *Archives of Diseases in Childhood*, 1995; 72, No. 3:198–203

Guidelines on the Nutritional Assessment of Infant Formulas, COMA report, HMSO, London, 1996

'Breastfeeding, Dummy Use, and Adult Intelligence', C.R. Gale, C.N. Martyn, MRC Environmental Epidemiology Unit, University of Southampton, Southampton General Hospital, *Lancet*, 1996, 347:1072–5

'Relation Between Early Introduction of Solid Food to Infants and Their Weight and Illnesses during the First Two Years of Life', J. Stewart Forsyth, S. Ogston, A. Clark, C. du V. Florey, P.W. Howie, *BMJ*, 1993, 306:1572–6

Weaning and the Weaning Diet, Report of the Committee on Medical Aspects of Food Policy, HMSO, London, 1994

The Effect of Beta-carotene Supplementation on the Immune Function of Blood Monocytes, D. Hughes, A.J.A. Wright, P. Finglas, A.C.J. Peerless, A. Bailey, S.B. Astley, A.C. Pinder, S. Southon, Department of Nutrition, Diet and Health, and Department of Food Biophysics, Institute of Food Research, Norwich (research funded by Ministry of Agriculture, Fisheries and Food (MAFF), 1996

The Scientific Basis of Dental Health Education, Health Education Authority, 1989

'Hungry for a New Revolution', J. Seymour, *New Scientist*, 30 March 1996:34–7

Aflatoxin Contamination of Peanut Butter and Peanuts, Food Surveillance Information Sheet No. 45, 1994, Food Safety Directorate, MAFF

Aflatoxin Contamination of Peanut Butter and Peanuts, Food Surveillance Information Sheet No. 56, 1995, Food Safety Directorate, MAFF

Aflatoxin Surveillance of Retail and Imported Nuts, Nut Products, Dried Figs and Fig Products, Food Surveillance Information Sheet No. 81, 1996, Food Safety Directorate, MAFF

Phthalates in Infant Formulae, Food Surveillance Information Sheets No. 83, 1996, Food Safety Directorate, MAFF

Phthalates in Food, Food Surveillance Information Sheet No. 82, 1996, Food Safety Directorate, MAFF

'The Potential Adverse Effects of Soyabean Phytoestrogens in Infant Feeding', C. Irvine, M. Fitzpatrick, I. Robertson, D. Woodhams, *New Zealand Medical Journal*, 1996, 108:208

Dioxins in Human Milk, Food Surveillance Information Sheet No. 88, May 1996, Food Safety Directorate, MAFF

'The Saccharin Generation', *The Food Magazine*, January/March 1996 *Sweetness and Lite*, a Food Commission survey of the increasing use of artificial sweeteners in UK food products, January 1996

1995 Survey of Apple Juice for Patulin, Food Surveillance Information Sheet No. 74, 1995, Food Safety Directorate, MAFF

'Cow's Milk and IDDM', Leonard C. Harrison, *Lancet*, 1996, 348:905–6

'Cell-mediated Immune Response to B Casein in Recent-onset Insulin-dependent Diabetes: implications for disease pathogenesis', M. Cavallo, D. Fava, L. Monetini, F. Barone, P. Pozzill, *Lancet*, 1996, 348:926–8

'Cow's Milk and Type 1 Childhood Diabetes: no increase in risk', M.J. Boddington, P.G. McNally, A.C. Burden, *Diabetic Medicine*, 1994, 11:663–5

'Early Infant Diets and Insulin-dependent Diabetes Mellitus', M.A. Atkinson, *Lancet*, 1996, 347:1464–5

Morbidity from Excessive Intake of High Energy Fluids: the Squash Drink Syndrome J.O'B. Hourihane, C.J. Rolles, Archives of Diseases in Childhood, 1995; 72, no. 2:141–3

'Is Water Out of Vogue: Survey of the Drinking Habits of 2–7 years olds' L.P.M. Peter et al, *Archives of Diseases in Childhood*, 1995; 72, no. 2:137–140

Report of the Working Party on Pesticide Residues in Food, 1995, MAFF

The Effect of Pesticides on Child Health, American National Research Council, 1993, Report of the Board on Agriculture, Environmental Studies and Toxicology's five-year study

Analysis of Lindane in Milk Samples 1995, Pesticides Safety Directorate, Report of the Working Party on Pesticide Residues, April 1996

Advisory Committee on Pesticides recommendations to MAFF, *Food Safety Information Bulletin*, January 1995

Nitrate in Vegetables, Food Surveillance Information Sheet No. 91, 1996, Food Safety Directorate, MAFF

Multi-element Analysis of Infant Foods – Follow-up Survey, Food Surveillance Information Sheet No. 93, 1996, Food Safety Directorate, MAFF

Useful Addresses

The following organisations can offer you help and information on various aspects of pregnancy, childcare and nutrition, as indicated. Some recommended books and magazines are also included here.

Chapter 1: Pregnancy

HERBS AND HERBALISTS

National Institute of Medical Herbalists
56 Longbrook Street
Exeter
EX4 6AH
tel. 01392 426022
Will supply the name of your nearest practitioner, or, if you send a stamped (31p) addressed 9 × 6 inch envelope, a complete directory of practitioners in the UK

The Complete Woman's Herbal by Anne McIntyre, published by Gaia, £15 from bookshops, offers helpful information on herbal products in general

FOLIC ACID AND PLANNING A PREGNANCY

Health Information Service
freephone 0800 66 55 44

NUTRITION DURING PREGNANCY

Sainsbury's/Wellbeing Eating for Pregnancy Helpline
Centre for Pregnancy Nutrition
University of Sheffield
Department of Obstetrics and Gynaecology
Northern General Hospital
Herries Road
Sheffield
S5 7AU
tel. 0114 242 4084 (24 hours)
Leaflets available

GIVING UP SMOKING DURING PREGNANCY

Quitline
tel. freephone 0800 00 22 00

SPINA BIFIDA

Association for Spina Bifida and Hydrocephalus (ASBAH)
ASBAH House
42 Park Road
Peterborough
PE1 2UQ
tel. 01733 555988

DIABETES

British Diabetic Association
10 Queen Anne Street
London W1M OBD
tel. 0171 323 1531
Publishes magazine *Pregnancy, Diabetes and You*, available from above address. A book, *Pregnancy and Diabetes*, by Bonnie Estridge and Jo Davies, is also available from the same address, price £8.99

Chapter 2: Breastfeeding

FEEDING

La Leche League
PO Box 29
West Bridgeford
Nottingham
NG2 7NP
or
PO Box BM 3424
London WC1N 3XX
tel. 0171 242 1278 for your local contact
Leaflets and three booklets, *A Mother's Guide to Milk Expression and Breast Pumps*, *Breastfeeding Your Baby, a Guide for Working Mothers* and *Marmet Technique for Manual Expression of Breast Milk*, are all available from the above addresses

National Childbirth Trust
Alexandra House
Oldham Terrace
London W3 6NH
tel. 0181 992 8637
The National Childbirth Trust Book of Breast-feeding by Mary Smale, published by Vermilion at £7.99, is available from bookshops or the above address

Association of Breastfeeding Mothers
Sydenham Green Health Centre
26 Holnshaw Close
London SE26 4TH
tel. 0181 778 4769
or contact your local branch (see telephone directory)

Other useful information on breastfeeding can be found in *Breast-feeding, You and Your Baby: a brief guide to breastfeeding,*

available free from:
Department of Health
PO Box 410
Wetherby
LS23 7LN

Baby Milk Action
23 St Andrew's Street
Cambridge
CB2 3AX
tel. 01223 464420

See also information under Herbs and Herbalists (Chapter 1, above)

CRYING BABIES

CRY-SIS
tel. 0171 404 5011

Chapter 3: Weaning

COMMERCIAL BABY FOODS

Baby Organix range
freephone 0800 393511

Boots' range
Ask to talk to the baby consultant (larger branches only)

Cow & Gate Baby-feeding Information Service
tel. 01345 623623

Hipp organic range
freephone 0800 4488222

Original Fresh Babyfood range
tel. 0141 332 0606

FIRST AID

First Aid for Children Fast, published by Dorling Kindersley in association with the British Red Cross, and available from bookshops price £7.99, is a good manual to keep handy

VEGETARIAN AND VEGAN BABIES

The Vegetarian Society
Parkdale
Dunham Road
Altrincham
Cheshire
WA14 4QG
tel. 0161 928 0793
Send a stamped addressed envelope for leaflets

The Vegan Society
7 Battle Road
St Leonards-on-Sea
East Sussex
TN37 7AA
tel. 01424 427393
Send a stamped addressed envelope for leaflets

TWINS

Twins and Multiple Births Association
PO Box 30
Little Sutton
South Wirral
Liverpool
L66 1TH

Chapter 5: Food Scares

ALLERGIES

British Allergy Foundation Helpline
tel. 0171 600 6166 (Mon–Fri 10a.m.–3p.m.)

The Anaphylaxis Campaign
PO Box 149
Fleet
Hampshire
GU13 9XU
tel. 01252 318723

Action Against Allergy
PO Box 278
Twickenham
Middlesex
TW1 4QQ
No telephone number for public; send a stamped addressed envelope
for leaflets

British Society of Allergy and Clinical Immunology
tel. 0181 398 9240
Not for the general public, but your GP can obtain a list of NHS
allergy clinics from the above address

British Dietetic Association
7th Floor
Elizabeth House
22 Suffolk Street
Queensway
Birmingham
B1 1LS
tel. 0121 643 5483

HORMONES IN FOOD AND RELATED ISSUES

To raise a matter with your local MP contact him or her at:
House of Commons
London SW1A 0AA
or look in Yellow Pages for the MP's local office address

Greenpeace
tel. 0171 865 8100

Friends of the Earth
tel. 0171 490 1555

Soil Association
Organic Food and Farming Centre
86 Colston Street
Bristol
BS1 5BB
tel. 0117 929 0661

Ministry of Agriculture (MAFF) Consumer Helpline
tel. 0345 573012 (calls charged at local rate) and MAFF
Food Safety Information Bulletin
tel. 0171 238 6335

The Food Commission
3rd Floor
Viking House
5–11 Worship Street
London EC2A 2BH
tel. 0171 628 7774
Publishers of *The Food Magazine*

Consumers' Association
2 Marylebone Road
London NW1 4DF
tel. 0171 830 6444
Publishers of magazine *Health Which?*

National Childbirth Trust
See under Feeding (Chapter 2, above)
Publishers of magazine *New Generation*

HERBAL DRINKS

National Institute of Medical Herbalists
See under Herbs and herbalists (Chapter 1, above)

HYPERACTIVE CHILDREN

Hyperactive Children's Support Group
71 Whyke Lane
Chichester
West Sussex
PO19 2LD
tel. 01903 725182
For a copy of *Hyperactive Children: a guide to their management*
send a stamped addressed envelope

PESTICIDES

Soil Association
See under Hormones etc. (this chapter, above)

Index

colic, 52–3
COMA (Committee on Medical Aspects
    of Food Policy) report on weaning,
    182
Committee on Toxicity of Chemicals in
    Food, Consumer Products and the
    Environment (COT), 176, 178,
    179–80
constipation, 45–6, 107
COT (Committee on Toxocity of
    Chemicals in Food, Consumer
    Products and the Environment), 176,
    178, 179–80
cot death, antimony in food and, 199
Creutzfeldt-Jakob disease *see* CJD
cyclamates, 180

dairy products, in pregnancy, 12
dental decay *see* teeth
Department of Health, 175, 177, 182
diabetes, 1, 3, 4
    bottle-feeding and, 184–5
    and pregnancy, 28–9
diarrhoea in babies, 53
dioxins in breastmilk, 178–9
docosahexaenoic acid (DHA), 48, 49
drinks, for babies, 77–9
    herbal, 87, 182–3
    and picky eaters, 104
    in pregnancy, 14
    see also fruit juice; soft drinks
dummies, 54–5, 88

eating disorders, 7
eggs, salmonella in, 199–200
essential fatty acids, 24
    in pregnancy, 12–13, 24
    in formula, 48
exercise, in pregnancy, 30

fish, 24, 49, 74
'floppy baby syndrome', 183–4
fluoride, 89
folic acid, 20, 21–2
Food Commission, 180
food intolerance (false food allergy),
    170–71
food safety rules, 109–110
food scares, 168–200
    antimony in food and cot death, 199
    bottle–feeding and diabetes, 184–5
    BSE ('Mad Cow disease'), 186–90

dioxins in breastmilk, 177–8
food allergy, 170–1
herbal drinks for babies and toddlers,
    182–3
honey ban for babies, 183–4
hormones in soya formula, 176–7
hyperactivity and diet, 185
nitrates in vegetables, 198
patulin in apple juice, 181–2
peanuts, 169–70, 171–74
pesticides, 191–8
phthalates in formula, 174–6
the risk from artificial sweeteners,
    179–81
salmonella in eggs and other food,
    199–200
squash can stunt children's growth,
    186
formula milk *see under* bottle–feeding
fruit
    children and, 2
    in pregnancy, 11
    washing, 193
fruit juice, 79, 86–7, 88, 89, 90
fruit squash, 79, 90, 186

growth, and fruit squash, 186

healthy diet
    babies, 74
    pregnancy, 10
heart attack, 2
heart disease, 1
herbal drinks, 87, 182–3
high blood pressure, 1, 2, 4
histamine, 171
honey, 183–4
Hyperactivity Children's Support Group,
    185
hyperactivity and diet, 185
hygiene, 109–10

insulin–dependent diabetes (IDDM), 28–
    9, 184
IQ (intelligence quotient), 3, 13, 33, 54–
    5, 107–8, 178
iron, 23, 108

LCPs *see* long chain fatty acids
let-down reflex, 39
lindane, 196
liver, 22, 25

teeth, 84–91
    and artificial sweeteners, 87, 89
    brushing, 89, 90, 91
    choice of toothbrush, 90
    and drinks, 79
    and fluoride, 89, 90, 91
    and fruit juice/soft drinks, 86–7,
        88, 89
    preventing tooth decay, 87–90
    step-by-step to healthy teeth,
        88–89
    and sugar, 85–6, 89, 90
    teething pains, 85
    tooth-friendly snacks, 91
'teething biscuits', 62
thaumatin, 87
toddlers
constipation, 107
    diet and IQ, 107–8
    eating up greens, 101–3
    one to two years, 94–8
    overweight, 106–7
    picky eaters, 103–6
    two to three years, 98–100
twins, 73

vegan diet, 7, 72
vegetable juices, 79
vegetables
    babies and, 6, 77
    children and, 2, 101–3
    nitrates in, 198
    in pregnancy, 11
    washing, 193
vegetarian and vegan babies, 72–3
vitamin A, 20, 22, 25–6, 83–4, 108
vitamin B, 2, 72
vitamin B1, 108
vitamin B2 (riboflavin), 20, 22, 72
vitamin B3 (niacin), 20, 108
vitamin B6, 108
vitamin B12, 20, 25, 72
vitamin C, 20, 22, 23, 108, 186
vitamin D, 20, 22, 83–4, 108

vitamin E, 24–5, 34
vitamin K, 36
vitamin supplements, 20, 82, 108

weaning, 56–108
    batch 'cooking', 66
    and breastfeeding, 35
    buying baby foods, 60–5
    commercially prepared baby foods,
        58–8
    drinks for babies, 78–9
    equipment, 65–6
    first tastes, 67–8
    food allergies, 69
    four to six months (stage 1), 57, 62,
        76–80
    from bottle to cup, 70
    heat and serve, 67
    home-made food, 59–60
    how to feed your baby, 75
    hygiene, 65
    month by month, 74
    nine months to a year, 57, 92–4
    overweight babies, 84–5
    premature babies, 71–2
    rusks or 'teething biscuits', 62
    safety first, 69
    self-feeding, 68
    six to nine months (stage 2), 57, 62,
        80–83
    storing baby food, 67
    timing the introduction of solids, 71
    tips for successful weaning, 75
    twins, 73
    vitamin supplements, 82
    weaning plan for 'at risk' infants, 69–
        70
    weaning step by step, 57–8
    weaning summary, 57, 70
    when to start, 70–71
Working Party on Pesticide Residues,
194, 198

yogurt, 61–2, 77

THE ABC OF HEALTHY EATING FOR BABIES AND TODDLERS